inside
baseball

inside baseball

revised edition

dell bethel

Contemporary Books, Inc.
Chicago

Library of Congress Cataloging in Publication Data

Bethel, Dell.
   Inside Baseball.

   Includes index.
   1. Baseball.   I. Title.
GV867.B46   1980   796.357'2   79-8738
ISBN 0-8092-7052-8

This book is dedicated to my wife, Polly, who is as splendid an assistant coach as a man could find, and to our son, Bill, the other outstanding assistant coach.

Published by Contemporary Books, Inc.
180 North Michigan Avenue, Chicago, Illinois 60601
Manufactured in the United States of America
Library of Congress Catalog Card Number: 79-8738
International Standard Book Number: 0-8092-7052-8

Published simultaneously in Canada by
Beaverbooks
953 Dillingham Road
Pickering, Ontario L1W 1Z7
Canada

contents

acknowledgments

I wish to acknowledge the great baseball players, coaches, and managers I have had the pleasure of playing under or working with side by side. Much of what is in this book I have learned from these men, who through their love and dedication have made baseball the great game it is today.

These men are William Leslie Bethel, Fred Warburton, Ray Ross, Ed Burke, Dick Siebert, Ray Gestaut, Angelo Giuliani, Andy Gilbert, Carl Hubbell, Bubber Jonnard, Paul Deese, Ron Oestrike, George Medich, Chick Genovese, Tom Heath, Jack Fisher, Leo Durocher, Don Kirsch, Cliff Dorow, John Kasper, Dave Kosher, Harvey Haddix, Larry Starr, Al Campanis, Galen Cisco, Grady Hatton, Jim Fitzharris, Rosy Ryan, Don Pries, Charlie Fox, Chuck Tanner, Rollie Hemond, Bill Veeck, Hal Middlesworth, Ed Katalinas, Rich Rollins, Ralph Kiner, Charlie Lau, John Sain, Wally Moses, Whitey Herzog, Dick Howser, George Brophy, Eddie Yost, Ray Berres, Brooks Robinson, Clete Boyer, Bud Harrelson, Mickey McConnell, Cliff Kachline, Harry Walker, Ted Williams, and Andy Cohen.

I also wish to express my sincere appreciation to Herman Masin, editor of *Scholastic Coach,* for his encouragement and assistance in my writing endeavors from the beginning.

With this revised edition of *Inside Baseball,* I deeply appreciate the cooperation and tremendous help from the Cleveland Indians Baseball Organization, especially Rich Rollins, Bob DiBiasio, Joe Bick, and Marshall Bossard. A real major league operation from top to bottom.

Big league photography in this book was taken by Marv Axelrod, Tony Foy, Sue Ogrocki, Tony Tomsic, and Paul Tepley —all big leaguers in their field.

Dell Bethel with Dick Howser, manager of the New York Yankees.

I have worked with Dell at baseball schools for several years and have found him to be a real student of baseball and a man who loves kids and teaching them baseball.

His ideas and methods of teaching baseball are a real look at *Inside Baseball*.

As a coach, Dell is a real teacher-coach, and his coaching record and players who have reached the major leagues speak for themselves.

Dell's coaching methods in the pages to follow will help you become a better baseball player.

Dick Howser
Manager of THE NEW YORK YANKEES

chapter 1
MECHANICS OF PITCHING

A high school coach can well afford to spend fifty percent of his time on his pitchers. Good pitching can compensate for weaknesses in every other department of the game, and it can make a winner out of an otherwise ordinary team.

There's no great secret to pitching. The basic problem is control. Control is more than the ability to throw in the strike zone; it also entails mastery of the corners and the low strike. The strike low and away comes closest to being the unhittable pitch.

Be relaxed at all times, both mentally and physically. To help yourself relax, take a deep breath before pitching. Know what pitch has been signalled for and where it should be thrown. Concentrate hard on delivering the pitch to that spot. If you can do this about one hundred times a game, you should be a consistent winner.

AIDS IN GAINING CONTROL

Try to split the heart of the plate with a low first pitch. If you have your good stuff, the ball should catch one of the corners.

Always throw at a target. This requires concentrated effort. Satchel Paige developed control by practicing with a safety matchbox for a plate. Another famous big leaguer tried pitching into a small can.

Visualize the anticipated path or groove of the pitch before delivering.

Start with the pivot foot on the middle of the rubber. If your pitch is wild inside or outside, simply move over on the rubber and keep using the same motion.

When you're wild high, you're releasing the ball too soon. When you're wild low, you're holding the ball too long.

Develop a groove so that your lead foot lands in the same spot every time. Carl Hubbell could warm up for twenty minutes and yet leave only one mark with his striding foot.

Throw each pitch from the same angle. Use your natural throwing motion on all pitches.

Work with one pitch at a time (first the fast ball, then the curve, etc.) until you can place it anywhere in the strike zone.

Learn to throw at the catcher's mitt,

In this great sequence of the stylish lefthander Rick Waits, find the basic principles and sound fundamentals of pitching we've been talking about in this chapter.

then his shoulders, knees, and finally the lettering on his uniform.

Use the plate in practice, throwing at the corners.

Know where every pitch is going and why it's going there.

Keep your head up and still.

Make a pitching target like the one shown here—two poles driven into the ground with strings tied to mark out the strike zone. Throw to the pitching "strings," using the bottom half of the strike zone only.

Draw a seven-foot line from your pivot foot toward home plate. On the delivery (if you're a right-handed pitcher) your left leg should always end up to the left of this line. This will prevent you from throwing across your body.

Have your coach show you how to use a John Sain Spinner to develop proper ball rotation (see Chapter 3).

Discipline yourself mentally. Anger destroys your concentration.

Throw the ball hard; don't aim it.

Run, run, and run some more. Lack of control late in the game is usually due to poor physical condition.

Check the wind conditions as soon as you arrive at the park. Wind at your back helps your fast ball. Wind directly in your face helps your curve.

Don't be "cute" or try to pitch in and out until you're ahead of the batter. Put something on the ball and get it over.

Talk to yourself on the mound; for example, say "low and outside" over and over. By doing this you shut out all distractions and concentrate your effort on improving your control.

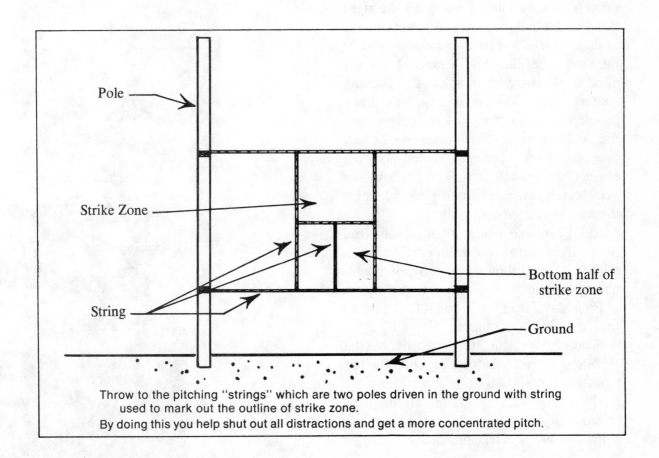

Throw to the pitching "strings" which are two poles driven in the ground with string used to mark out the outline of strike zone.
By doing this you help shut out all distractions and get a more concentrated pitch.

When your pitches are coming in higher than you want, aim at the hitter's shoe tops.

Dip the knee of your pivot leg; this gives you a chance to push off as you start your forward motion.

If you're tall you must dip the knee of your pivot leg to consistently keep the ball low. The dip lowers your projected trajectory and improves the follow-through of your arm and back. A lazy back leg produces high pitches.

Have your coach hold your pivot foot during practice. This will force you to keep your back leg close to the ground and thereby get your body and back into each pitch.

Your state of mind is a most important factor in control. Frank Sullivan, former pitching ace of the Red Sox and Twins, had this to say about mental preparedness:

"I try to get rid of all tension before going out to pitch. Thinking is the key to winning. You may know how to do the right thing on the mound, but you won't be able to do it unless you have command of your thinking apparatus. For instance, I free my mind of all worry about whom I'm pitching against, where I'm playing, or how many people are in the stands. I concentrate on the job I'm doing—which is getting the ball over the plate. The job is complicated, especially for a tall [6 ft. 7 in.] fellow like me. Relaxation, mental and physical, helps me concentrate on control."

San Francisco Giant pitchers solve the physical preparedness problem by maintaining the following "between-assignments" routine:

First day: Run, run, run—foul line to foul line. Repeat 14 times.

Second day: Run, throw easily on the sidelines, or pitch batting practice for ten minutes.

Third day: Throw about ten minutes (optional).

Fourth day: Pitch again.

Two keys to getting your body into the pitch are bending the back knee and loading up your weight (photos 6–11). Also, keep your front shoulder closed so you don't lose your body power. Guidry waits until photo 15 to open the front shoulder.

Ron Guidry, the classic lefthander who was the best pitcher in baseball in 1978, won 27 games and lost only 3. Ron has fantastic arm speed, somewhere between 600 to 700 miles per hour just before reaching his release point. His arm speed coupled with his ability to get his body totally behind the pitch in a very smooth, fluid, and powerful motion is why he is able to throw his fast ball up to speeds of 100 miles per hour even though he only weighs 155 pounds.

Notice how he really buries his pitching shoulder into the ground in photos 16, 17, and 18 from the wind-up and photo 13 from the stretch.

Also note how he literally explodes and jumps at the hitter, letting his whole body go into the pitch to get that little extra on each delivery. It is very apparent in photo 19 from the wind-up.
Being an all-around athlete (Ron has run the 100-yard dash in 9.7 seconds) and having great spring in his legs help him to do a splendid job of fielding his position. Note in the last photo from the wind-up and from the stretch his perfect fielding position. He is ready to spring like a cat in any direction, including straight up for a high hopper. Both photo sequences truly show poetry in motion. Especially note in photos 16-19 from the wind-up how freely the back leg is allowed to follow through with no strain on the body.

THE PITCHER'S MOTION

Good control starts with a good motion. The motion consists of (1) wind-up, (2) roll or lay-back, (3) delivery, and (4) follow-through.

Bob Shaw insists that the right-hander's roll shouldn't bring his shoulder farther around than in a direct line with the plate. John Sain feels that the roll can bring the shoulder around almost in line with second base. Each pitcher should experiment with the roll best suited for him. In general, though, the farther the roll, the longer the pitcher must lay back with his lead leg up. Pitchers should try to put their front hip pockets in the hitter's face. This develops an excellent *pitching rhythm* because the arm will not have to hurry to catch up with the front hip and leg.

Use a slow wind-up. All smooth pitchers start with a slow wind-up.

Get your forward leg up and hold it there until your pitching hand comes out of your glove with the ball (just after you raise your leg). As your forward leg begins to descend, your back leg should be sharply

flexed and your front hip pocket should be turned toward the hitter.

Next, thrust your pitching elbow out. Then, as your leg comes down in front of the mound, begin to uncoil your whole body, starting your forward swing. Your hand and forearm should be back and up, and your elbow should lead far ahead of your hand just before the release of the ball. This gives you a much more effective snap with your forearm and wrist. This whipping action is vital to the velocity you can impart to the ball.

Pitchers must know how to push off from the rubber (especially from the stretch position), as this also increases speed. In the stretch position, the pivot foot rests against the side of the rubber—which serves as a launching pad for the delivery. This compensates for the lack of the wind-up. Pitchers should "buggywhip" or whiplash their arms for extra snap.

The average stride is between four-and-a-half and five feet. Be careful not to overstride. Overstriding is one of the most common faults among young pitchers.

If your pitch is consistently high, shorten your stride. This enables you to get your arm down faster. If your pitch is consistently low, lengthen your stride. This allows you to release the ball sooner.

Mastery of the pitching art requires thousands of hours of practice and study. One major league team has figured that it takes some 12,000 hours of practice to create a real pitching prospect.

TYPES OF PITCHES

Fast Ball

For this pitch, the overhand pitcher generally grips the ball across the seams at their widest point. The seams will rotate against wind resistance to produce a "hopping" fast ball. A three-quarter arm pitcher (right-handed pitcher) uses the same grip, but his pitch will rise and go in on a right-handed hitter. A sidearmer's fast ball should move in and sink when gripped on the seams. Always remember that the index finger controls the direction of the fast ball.

A fastballer must reach back as far as possible to make his arm cover a larger arc and increase his leverage. A proper follow-through can increase speed by ten percent.

The wrist must be cocked for maximum speed, and the hand should be eighteen inches from the head when the ball is released. The final force is imparted by the fingers and wrist. A good snap will increase the velocity of the pitch.

Obviously, speed is the essence of the fast ball; so the push-off from the rubber, which increases speed, is especially important with this pitch, particularly in the

Fast Ball

Curve

Sinker

Note in these pictures of pitching grips the way the fingers are *hooked* around the baseball. It is important to keep the fingers in this hooked position right up to the time the ball is released, for maximum effectiveness.

stretch position. To recap what was said above, in the stretch position the pivot foot rests against the side of the rubber, which serves as a launching pad for the delivery. This compensates for the lack of wind-up. Pitchers should "buggywhip" their arms for extra snap.

Curve Ball

Although the curve is the most difficult pitch to learn, it pays the greatest dividends. The ball should be gripped on the seams, with the second finger imparting the all-important spin.

A John Sain Spinner can be used to demonstrate the proper spin (see Chapter 3). The correct action can also be practiced by constantly snapping a ball out of the hand with the thumb and second finger with a quick flipping motion. Another aid in learning to deliver a curve ball is to bring your pitching hand right over the top of your head as if you were parting your hair down the middle. This will help you get on top of the ball and insure good rotation, which is the mark of a fine curve ball.

In throwing a curve, the side (narrowest part) of the pitcher's forearm should be facing the hitter. This point is often neglected. The forearm motion is similar to

Notice in this sequence how Mike Flanagan has all the proper body mechanics of pitching right. In photo 1 he has his weight back. In photo 2 he is able to throw the ball in a downward plane, because his arm and hand are up high. His pivot foot (photo 3) is parallel with the rubber, which makes it harder to rush. His body (photo 4) is square with home plate. Notice in photo 4 that Flanagan brings his hands over his head, as does every outstanding pitcher. And notice in photo 6 how he pulls the pitching hand out of the glove so that he can get his hand up.

the movement used in pulling down a window shade directly in front of you.

The pitcher can get the feel of throwing a curve by imagining that he's driving nails into his foot. His elbow should be pulled in slightly and his hand should be about four inches away from his head as it comes by the bill of his cap, compared to eighteen inches away from his head on a fast ball. For the curve-ball pitch it's important to shorten the stride and not throw too hard.

Good wrist action is a necessity; it should be sharp, not lazy. Famous curve-baller Rosy Ryan believed that the pitcher's thumb and second finger should be snapped as the arm reaches the cap on the downward motion.

A good curve ball will disrupt the hitter's sighting plane as it breaks down. A batter who wears glasses can be pitched low to force him to look through the frames

Curves should be kept low and away. By adjusting or rotating the ball so that the middle finger is along the seam, the pitcher can make the curve come off the side of the index finger with all four seams rotating downward. On this delivery, the middle finger must grip the ball firmly. A pitcher having trouble getting "stuff" on his curves may be gripping the ball too tightly. It is also important to be sure you are *hooking* your fingers around the ball, which makes it possible to get maximum spin on the ball.

In this unusual pitching sequence of Randy Lerch, we are looking at the pitcher from the hitter's point of view. Notice how Lerch keeps his shoulders closed and straight, which allows him to get his maximum power into the pitch.

Change-of-Pace

The change-of-pace or change-up pitch may be thrown in one of two ways. The pitcher may simply jam the ball far back into his hand, thereby taking something off the pitch, or he may remove his two fingers from the ball just before the release to brake the ball's action.

The slower the pitch, the harder it is to hit for distance, since speed of a hit depends greatly on the impact of bat on ball, which imparts an "equal and opposite" force on the ball. A good change-up will be effective in throwing a hitter's timing off.

ANALYSIS OF GREAT PITCHERS

Having discussed the mechanics of pitching, let's get the thinking of three great pitchers.

Whitey Ford's thinking is simply this: He attempts to put the ball where he wants it and where he hopes the batter doesn't want it. He throws the curve inside, the fast ball outside, then brings the fast ball in and sends the curve out. He moves the ball around, changes speeds. He doesn't try to throw strikes over the middle of the plate.

The difference between pitchers and throwers is control, Ford says. If the pitcher can get the first pitch over with good stuff on it, he has an edge. The hitter then has to go chasing.

The big secret in throwing an outstanding knuckle ball is the release. In these pictures of Wilbur Wood, one of the greatest knuckle-ball pitchers of all time (now retired), the high-powered camera shows us why. The key to throwing a knuckle ball is to come to your release point and then imagine you're just pushing a door open with your hand as you release the ball. Notice in photo 3 how Wood is coming to that point, and then he will just push his hand through and relax it in photo 5. Note in photo 1 how his fingers are dug into the ball.

As long as a pitcher is on the mound, he should feel he's the boss. Only he knows what he's throwing and where he's throwing it. And when the batter guesses right, he still has to hit the ball. A craftsman will stop him three out of four times. "I will never give in to a hitter with a runner in scoring position."

Carl Erskine's ideas, though somewhat different from Ford's, are fundamental and sound. Carl believes an outstanding pitcher must have the ability to concentrate intensely. For example, if someone came out to the mound and asked the pitcher his phone number, the good pitcher often wouldn't be able to tell it to him, he'd be concentrating on his job so completely.

The pitcher must acquire as much knowledge as possible. He must understand that finger pressure affects pitching speed and that different spins provide different curves. The angle of the spin gives direction to the curve.

For Erskine, tilting the angle of spin to one side on a fast-pitched ball made it rise or sail to that side as it reached the plate. Erskine found that by pressing more with one finger than another he affected the angle of the backspin. Then he noticed that shifting the pressure points—pulling the first finger back a bit and then pulling the second finger back—tilted the angle of spin to either inside or outside.

The main thing for a pitcher to learn about a batter is whether he's a low ball or high ball hitter, Erskine says. Then the pitcher can determine how to pitch him.

Ed Lopat became great even though he had short fingers and couldn't throw very hard. He was a thinking pitcher, and

The Perfect Pitch: If you're not in the position shown in photo 2, you have done something wrong in your basic pitching mechanics. In photo 3 you see the actual release point, right by the ear. Note ball is released before head. The pitcher's pitching shoulder is buried in the ground, insuring a good follow-through.

youngsters would do well to adopt his approach and methods.

Lopat says: "Take four pitches—the fast ball, the curve, the slider, and the screwball. Now throw these at different speeds, and you have twelve pitches. Next, throw each of those twelve pitches with a long-armed or short-armed motion, and you have twenty-four pitches."

This is why batters could never dig in against Lopat. The average pitcher who had to get the ball over the plate could be counted on to come in with one or perhaps two pet pitches; Lopat could choose any one of two dozen.

Taken individually, none of these pitches was really a "big pitch." Each looked easy to hit; their effectiveness lay in numbers.

"My main objective," Lopat says, "was to keep the batter hitting off-stride. If I could do that, I felt I had the hitters beaten. They might get a lot of plunkers, but that was about all."

In discussing pitching, Lopat often refers to the "power zone." This is the point over the plate where the batter's swing achieves the peak of its power. Lopat, with his deceptive motion and varying speeds, lured the batters into meeting the ball as much as three inches in front of or behind that point of maximum power.

Lopat threw between 90 to 130 pitches a game. He realized that he was bound to throw a few bad ones out of this number, but he tried his hardest not to throw a bad one in situations where it would do the most damage or to hitters who could swat the ball into the seats.

In Lopat's mind, pitching comes down to a battle of wits between the pitcher and the batter in which a single mistake can cost a game.

"You have to find out how the hitter thinks, as well as how he swings," Lopat says. "The tip-off to his thinking lies in his reflexes. If I threw a batter a fast ball and he just ticked it, I knew he wasn't looking for a fast ball. Then I might throw him another fast ball, depending on where the first ball was thrown. Now, if you get a smart hitter out with a pitch, and you give it to him when he's at bat again with less than two strikes on him, you're crazy. After two strikes your chances of striking out the batter are better because he has to protect the plate, and he can't take a full swing."

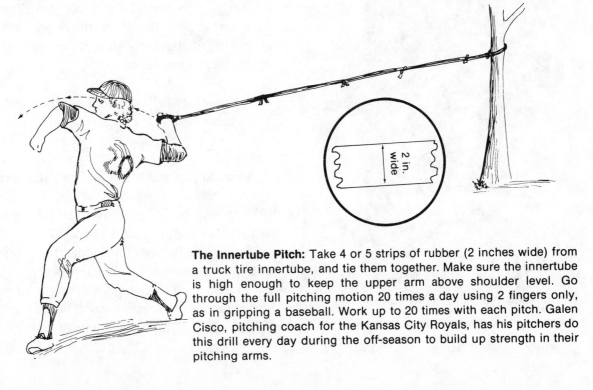

The Innertube Pitch: Take 4 or 5 strips of rubber (2 inches wide) from a truck tire innertube, and tie them together. Make sure the innertube is high enough to keep the upper arm above shoulder level. Go through the full pitching motion 20 times a day using 2 fingers only, as in gripping a baseball. Work up to 20 times with each pitch. Galen Cisco, pitching coach for the Kansas City Royals, has his pitchers do this drill every day during the off-season to build up strength in their pitching arms.

chapter 2
HARVEY HADDIX ON PITCHING

Harvey Haddix is a master craftsman who accomplished the near impossible in pitching twelve perfect innings, thirty-six

Harvey Haddix, major league pitching coach.

men retired in order—still a record today.

Today he has become an outstanding and respected pitching coach in the major leagues and a master of teaching pitchers how to set up a hitter and how to throw a change of pace. He is also the master of pitching mechanics and of showing a pitcher how to correct the habit of rushing. Len Barker and Jim Bibby have both said he contributed greatly in making them top major league pitchers.

Harvey, what did you do as a youngster that helped you become an outstanding pitcher and one of the best all-time fielding pitchers?

As a kid I would throw balls by the hour against cement steps and would learn to field ground balls, line drives, and fly balls as they came off the back steps. This really made me as a fielder. Throwing at the steps as a kid also helped me develop as a youngster. I also used to swing an 8- to 16-pound sledgehammer over my head. This not only helped me develop arm strength, but as I developed in the pro's, it helped to keep my shoulders free of injury.

In what ways did being a splendid (Golden Glove) fielding pitcher help, besides the obvious?

On a major league level the biggest advantage to the team is that the manager can play his shortstop more to the third base side and have the second baseman shade more toward first, knowing that his man on the mound will get most anything hit up the middle.

In the world of baseball you are considered one of the best in teaching a pitcher how to set up a hitter and work on him. What is your thinking on this?

Setting up a hitter is a real art. The basic ideas I like to teach are, first, get ahead of the hitter. Second, I'm a firm believer that eighty-five percent of the game should be pitched on the outside corner of the plate. Third, if you're going to pitch inside, be sure to pitch *way inside.*

As a pitcher develops in the fine points of the game, I like him to throw his change-up from the knees into the dirt and the curve ball low and outside, *rather than take his heater (fast ball) and move it around in the strike zone.*

Location is vital in a pitching sequence. I prefer to have the first pitch a low and away fast ball.

Catfish Hunter is a splendid example of a great control pitcher. Often he would start a hitter off down the pipe. Then Catfish would divide the plate in halves and work the entire game on the outside half of the plate. Also, in a tight situation you should go with your best pitch. Go with your strength even if it is the hitter's strength. That to me is a great philosophy —pitch your game on the outer half of the plate. Bust the pitch on the hitter's hands, and then go outside.

You had a great change-of-pace as a pitcher and have had fantastic success in teaching it to major league pitchers. How do you teach it?

It is very important with the change-up to *keep it low,* from the knee to the dirt. One of the secrets in throwing the change-of-pace is to lead with the elbow which helps you to keep good arm speed, because a slow arm speed will tip the hitter off too soon that a change-up is coming. Then bring the ball in front of your body before releasing it. Bring your pitching hand down like a Big Sis Slap Down, and reach out with a *limp hand* as you release the ball.

What do you feel are the basic mechanics of pitching, and how do you teach them?

The first thing is that most young pitchers don't realize that they *can stand flat-footed,* reach back, and throw at almost their full speed without a wind-up or a step. Once a pitcher understands this, we can start teaching him a great deal.

I feel a pitcher needs certain physical characteristics: (1) quick feet, (2) strong forearms, (3) strong hands, and (4) on the mental side of the ledger, the potentiality of becoming a great competitor.

Eighty-Five percent of pitching troubles are the result of a pitcher rushing, even at the major league level.

What is rushing? How do you correct it? I know that when you were pitching coach with the Cleveland Indians, you and Jeff Torborg worked with Len Barker (who had lost his heater because of rushing) and helped him get it back.

Rushing is the biggest fault in pitching. What happens is while the pitching arm is still going back, the body starts moving forward. This mistake will keep you from developing proper timing and maximum power because the only way the arm can catch up is by dropping down. Rushing will also limit your ability to develop good breaking balls because your arm drops below shoulder level, preventing you from being on top of the ball.

One way to correct rushing is by starting with a slow wind-up. This enables you to increase gradually to full acceleration. Step straight back with your rear leg. Bring your front knee up close to the rubber for balance. Reach back with your *arm, and as it comes up to its peak, then start the body forward.* Keep your front shoulder in, don't open it too soon or turn it too far back as this will destroy your aim and also cause a loss of power in your pitch. *Never go forward* until your hand reaches its peak.

To summarize: (1) bring your leg under you; (2) relax your wrist; (3) slow down your wind-up; (4) Rushing is eighty-five percent of a pitcher's trouble. Stay within yourself. *Don't try to be better than you are.*

Another fundamental is to break your hands and bring your arm back. Don't bring the glove back. Throw with one hand, and grip the ball softly since a tight grip increases friction. Then at the release point really *flip* the baseball rather than throw it. When shooting for the outside corner, have the catcher move outside with his body so that you can use his body for a target.

In this unique sequence of Sparky Lyle, now with the Texas Rangers, we are able to see how he throws his fantastic sinking slider.

The slider curves sharply to the side with more velocity than a curve ball. Notice in photos 11, 12, and 13 how Lyle lays back, giving his arm plenty of time to start forward while not rushing his body. Photos 14 and 15 show the key to his great slider. His fingers and hand are on top of the ball, his arm is high, and notice that his wrist is stiff, perfectly straight with the arm.

How do you teach a pitcher to throw a slider or a sinking slider the way Sparky Lyle, Ron Guidry, and Sid Monge do so effectively?

To throw their kind of slider grip the ball like a sinker—where the narrowest part of the seams come together. Holding your two fingers together and on *top of the ball* will make your slider sink. Throw the slider as hard as you want, as long as you keep your fingers and hand on top of the ball, as Lyle does. *Hold your wrist perfectly straight in a line with your forearm and wrist.* There should be no break in the wrist at all (no wrist snap) while you throw. This is hard for young pitchers to learn. Then, as you get to your release point (in between the release points for a fast ball and breaking pitch), you should pull straight down hard just as if you're pulling a window shade down in front of you. This will give you the great sinking action that Lyle and Guidry have perfected.

TO SUMMARIZE—THE GREAT SLIDER

1. Grip ball on two narrow seams with fingers together.
2. Keep fingers and hand on top of the baseball.
3. Hold hand and wrist in a straight line with the forearm, no break or lay back in wrist.
4. Get the upper arm above the shoulder, and stay on top of the ball.
5. Release the ball by pulling hard straight down in front of you as in pulling a window shade down.

chapter 3
JOHN SAIN ON PITCHING

The first thing a major-league baseball scout looks for in a pitcher is the speed of his fast ball. With rare exception, a boy must have a strong arm and a fast fast ball to rate a chance for the majors. Speed is the one quality nobody can teach him. He either has it or he hasn't, although he might slightly improve it with better mechanics.

Important as it is, however, speed isn't all there is to pitching success. Few pitchers can get by in fast company with just a fast ball. The young pitcher must also develop control, a curve ball, and a change-of-pace pitch. And in time, as his arm starts losing its elasticity or the batters start catching up with his basic pitches, the smart hurler will have to develop an extra pitch—a slider, a sinker, a screwball, or some offbeat pitch.

The moral is: Any young pitcher who wants to get anywhere in baseball shouldn't rely on only one good pitch—unless, perhaps, he can throw the ball as hard as a Walter Johnson or pitch "butterflies" (knuckleballs) like a Hoyt Wilhelm. The more rounded his pitching repertoire, the better his chances for advancement.

Also, the earlier a boy begins learning to throw various pitches, the better. The high school coach might immediately protest:

John Sain

"Do you mean you want me to teach my kids to throw sliders, sinkers, and knucklers?"

My answer is yes—with reservations. I realize most coaches and trainers discourage youngsters from fooling around with "freak" deliveries. They believe that the young arm isn't strong enough to be strained in this fashion, and that it might be permanently injured. They also believe that a boy at this age should be concentrating wholly on control of his basic pitches.

This reasoning is sound—as far as it goes. But I believe this: The earlier a boy starts learning anything, the sooner he is going to master it.

Why wait until a boy is eighteen or nineteen before teaching him the mechanics of the various types of breaking pitches? You'll be retarding his progress. He's going to need one or more of these pitches in the not-so-distant future, and instead of having them at his command at that time, he's going to have to start learning them.

I don't mean that a twelve-, thirteen- or fourteen-year-old boy should be sent out on the mound and started on curve-ball pitching. I do mean that he should be given an understanding of the proper mechanics of all pitches—why rotation is important, how it is applied, what it does to the ball.

How can this be done? For a long time I used to demonstrate rotation by holding a ball in my left hand and showing the various types of spin with the other. This left something to be desired. The different mechanical actions and rotations were not only difficult to demonstrate, but could hardly be remembered, much less practiced without abusing the arm.

One afternoon I noticed Ralph Terry on the bench practicing spin by flipping the ball in various ways. I said, "Ralph, I'm going to fix up a ball so that you can spin it a whole lot easier and better than that."

John Sain's Spinner

Thinking about it on the way home, an idea occurred to me. When I got home I went into the living room, picked an apple out of the fruit bowl, then plucked the end out of one of the rabbit ears (indoor antenna) of my TV set. I stuck the thin bar through the apple and now I had a "baseball" I could spin to my heart's content. The next step was the development of the Spinner shown in the drawing.

With this Spinner, I feel that every boy can practice the correct way of spinning a baseball for all types of pitches. Of course, this sort of practice won't guarantee that a boy can go out the next day and start snapping off sharp-breaking curves, rising fast balls, and deceptive sinkers. But it will give him an understanding of the spin he must apply to make the ball do these things.

It's the spin that makes a curve ball curve, a slider slide, a sinker and a screwball sink, and a fast ball rise. And always remember: Good-breaking pitches must go down.

LEARNING THE CURVE-BALL PITCH

At one time a distinction was made between curves and "drops." The curve was usually a flat-breaking pitch, while the "drop" did just that, it dropped. The distinction has long vanished. Since a flat curve isn't usually effective, the good curve ball breaks downward. In short, a curve ball—in modern parlance—is a breaking pitch that goes down.

The reason is simple enough. If a curve stays on a horizontal plane, the batter's visual line won't be too badly disconcerted. Even if he's fooled by the pitch, he can continue to bring his bat around on a horizontal plane—pulling it in or reaching out —to meet the ball. When the ball sinks, however, the batter's visual line must suddenly change from the horizontal to the vertical. And if he has been bringing his bat around on a horizontal plane, he'll have to quickly dip it to meet the ball. That takes some doing, particularly if he already has committed himself to a flat swing.

The "hanging curve," which is so often hit out of the park, is merely a curve that hasn't been spun sharply enough to make it drop.

Every good curve-ball pitcher I know has told me he started throwing curves at an early age. Most of us started by spinning the ball with extreme caution and with as little strain on the arm as possible, until the muscles were coordinated and strong enough for the actual execution.

The secret lies in careful planning: (1) giving the boy a thorough understanding of the mechanics, (2) starting him slowly, having him merely spin the ball at half-speed, (3) seeing that he warms up properly before attempting any hard throws, (4) making sure he has the coordination and strength to attempt these pitches, (5) supervising him carefully to see that he doesn't abuse his arm.

Always remember this about that last point: A boy can hurt his arm throwing

fast balls just as easily as he can throwing curve balls.

How do you develop a smooth delivery? With nobody on base, take a stance squarely facing the batter. Place your front spike over the edge of the rubber, slightly angled to the right to facilitate the pivot. Set the other (striding) foot a few inches back of the rubber. Keep your body fairly erect, with your weight forward and shoulders level. When taking the sign, hide the ball from the batter. You may place it behind the thigh of the front foot. A short wind-up—one or at most two pumps— loosens the arm and helps bring the weight behind the pitch. Swing your arms up past your hips and join them overhead, making sure to keep the back of your glove turned toward the hitter—thus concealing the ball from him.

Now the pivot begins. Slide your pitching (front) foot diagonally forward into the hole and turn your body to the right. Then, as your arm goes back, swing your left leg up and around so that you face the batter over your left shoulder. Don't kick your left leg too high; it may throw you off balance. As you can see, you're now in a perfectly balanced position; in fact, at this point you should be able to come to a stop without falling either forward or backward.

Just before bringing your pitching arm forward, start the downward stride with your left leg. Hit the ground with it flatly, not on your heel, and point your toe directly at the plate. Your arm is brought through in a free, easy, but powerful motion, with your weight flowing from rear to front foot—the unwinding of hips providing both momentum and power. In releasing the ball, have a quick forearm and wrist action. This is important for all pitches. Don't stop jerkily after the ball leaves your hand. Bend your back and let your arm relax as soon as the ball is released, thus relieving the tension on the entire arm. As your arm follows through to the opposite side, your right leg comes forward in a squared-off position and your glove is brought around to the front of your body. You're now in perfect fielding position—ready to move right, left, or forward with equal facility.

From start to finish of the delivery, your head should remain fixed. It should not move or be thrown from side to side or up and down. Take a look at some of the pitching sequences in Chapter 1 to see how the professionals do this.

USE OF THE BASEBALL SPINNER

The handle is held in the nonpitching hand while the proper spin on the ball is sharply imparted with the pitching hand. The direction in which the handle is pointed is of vital importance, since it puts the ball in the correct axis for the specific type of delivery and spin.

The grip should be light but firm, not tight, with the two top fingers fairly close together and the thumb directly underneath them. A too-firm grip tightens the muscles on the underside of the forearm, partly locking the wrist. And if there's anything that a good curve-ball pitcher needs, it's a flexible wrist to get the necessary spin on the ball.

The drawings show how the Spinner can be used by any type of pitcher—overhand, three-quarter, and sidearm. They demonstrate the correct axis for each type of spin, as well as the direction in which the spin should be applied (arrows).

Fast ball

Holding the Spinner in the position shown in the drawings, apply the spin in the direction indicated by the arrow. This will make the ball rotate back toward you.

It's the speed and spin that make a fast ball move or hop. The really good overhand fast ball will level off or rise. The three-quarter or sidearm delivery, when thrown with good enough speed and spin, will move in on the hitter (right-handed pitcher to right-handed hitter, or left-handed pitcher to left-handed hitter).

While a fast ball can sometimes be improved through practice and the development of coordination, the best fast balls seem to be rare gifts of nature.

Curve

Check the direction of the Spinner handle for the proper axis. Hook your fingers around the ball and then sharply apply spin in the direction of the arrow in the drawing.

Most pitchers apply this spin by simultaneously pulling down with the fingers and flipping up with the thumb, spinning the ball in the direction of the arrow. The coordination of these two movements should give the youngster a faster rotation. He can try spinning the ball with only top fingers, using a light pull downward in the direction of the arrow. Next, he can try flipping the ball upward, using only the thumb.

After learning to get good rotation on the Spinner, don't immediately start on sharp breaking curves. After a preliminary warm-up, try throwing about half-speed, applying the spin you've learned on the Spinner. Since you no longer have the ball on a handle, you must watch the spin while the ball is in flight. In your early attempts, be satisfied if the ball merely spins in the right direction, even if it doesn't curve.

Before trying to throw faster and sharper breaking curves, make sure you have a smooth delivery and that there's little strain on your arm. As mentioned before, the mechanics should be learned at about half-speed. Most arms are hurt when a

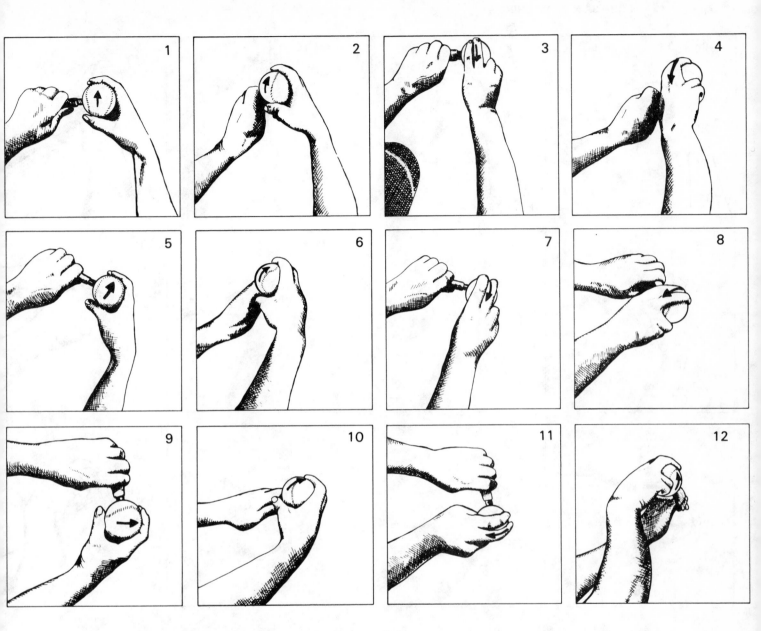

The positions for hands for right-handed pitchers: curve ball, slider, fast ball, and sinker.

1. Overhand curve ball
2. Overhand slider
3. Overhand fast ball
4. Three-quarter sinker
5. Three-quarter curve ball
6. Three-quarter fast ball
7. Three-quarter fast ball
8. Side-arm sinker
9. Side-arm curve ball
10. Side-arm slider
11. Side-arm fast ball
12. Screwball

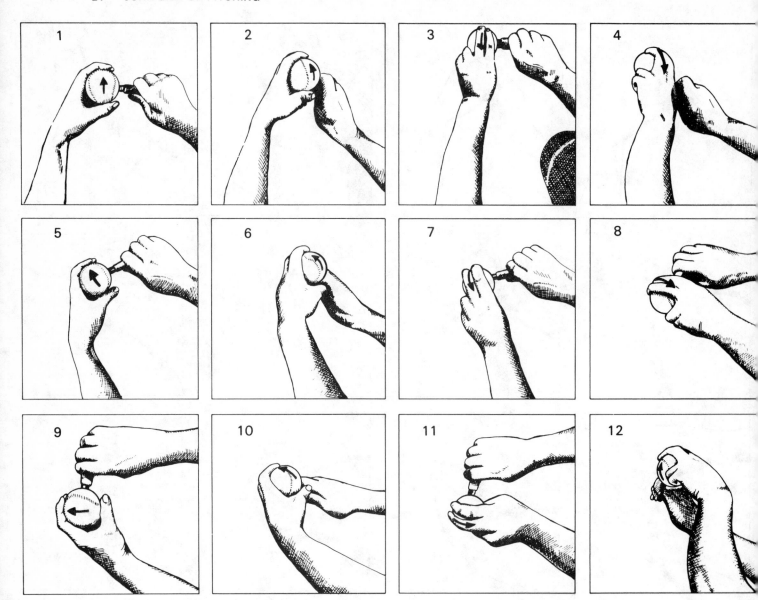

The positions for hands for left-handed pitchers: curve ball, slider, fast ball, and sinker.

1. Overhand curve ball
2. Overhand slider
3. Overhand fast ball
4. Three-quarter sinker
5. Three-quarter curve ball
6. Three-quarter slider
7. Three-quarter fast ball
8. Side-arm sinker
9. Side-arm curve ball
10. Side-arm slider
11. Side-arm fast ball
12. Screwball

pitcher starts losing his temper, showing off, or throwing hard without a proper warm-up.

Slider (fast curve)

The slider is really a fast ball with a break at the end. The break may take a little off its speed, but it's a highly effective pitch to go along with the regular fast ball, curve, and change-up.

The axis, or handle, of the Spinner is now pointed downward and to the left side of the plate for a right-handed pitcher, and downward in the direction of the break. (The left-handed pitcher holds the Spinner just the opposite; that is, toward the right of the plate.) Apply the spin by *pulling down* in the direction of the arrow. This produces an off-center fast-ball spin whose axis is downward in the direction of the break.

If this doesn't work for you, experiment with your own ideas. Just remember that most mechanical pitches should be practiced at about half-speed and that you should wait until you're coordinated and understand the mechanics before trying to make a pitch break sharply.

Sinker

Compare the three-quarter sinker and the three-quarter fast ball drawings. You'll notice that the axis in the sinker is downward and slightly forward as the fast-ball spin is imparted. The turning of the wrist produces a loss of some forward speed, which is why a sinker is slightly slower than a fast ball. In throwing the sinker it is important to bring your whole arm across your body and to the outside of the opposite knee.

Now compare the sidearm sinker and the sidearm fast ball drawings. Again note the axis change, and how the fast-ball spin is applied in both instances.

Screwball

This is a very difficult pitch to learn and be consistent with. The ball acts like a reverse curve, moving out and down when delivered by a left-handed pitcher to a right-handed hitter, or by a right-handed pitcher to a left-handed hitter. It is produced by a combination of spin, change of speed and motion, and to be effective, these three factors must be properly coordinated.

Compare the three-quarter screwball and the three-quarter fast ball drawings. Notice that the axis changes slightly in each, creating a change in the wrist position. Since the wrist and forearm are sharply turned in—an unnatural action—most people believe that the screwball puts a lot of strain on the arm. This strain can be reduced by proper mechanics and delivery. This applies to all mechanical pitches, plus the fast ball. If the pitcher can't tell when he's abusing his arm, a coach or some other knowledgeable baseball man must supervise his throwing.

(You may purchase a Spinner by writing: Training Aids Unlimited, 1033 Broadway, Denver, Colorado 80203.)

John Sain has many creative ideas about other phases of pitching. Here are some of those ideas, discussed during a question-and-answer session between the author and Coach Sain.

John, what method would you use to develop a young pitcher?

First I like to find a boy's natural way of throwing. One way of finding this is to hit fungos to him in the outfield and watch him throw the ball back. Generally this will be his natural way of throwing and the way he should pitch. The next step is to develop a smooth pitching motion that will allow freedom of movement and rhythm. Most sore arms come from ignoring this principle and abusing the arm.

How do you feel a pitcher should get ready for spring training, especially in a winter climate?

Two drills that I think make a boy ready or nearly ready for spring training are bench jumping and the cement block exercise.

In the bench or chair jumping exercise the pitcher faces the bench, which is about three feet in height. He jumps and places one foot on the bench, keeping his weight on the foot on the floor. Then he jumps again, exchanging feet and placing the opposite foot on the bench. This exercise should also be done with the boy standing parallel to the bench and jumping, alternating his legs. He should repeat this rapidly fifty times. This exercise builds up a pitcher's legs.

The cement block drill is one that can be used in your basement, gym or small area, and you don't need a catcher. This makes it possible to work on your arm and various pitches. Obtain a three-foot-square cement block with one side smooth (so it doesn't scuff your baseballs up). It should be fairly thick so the impact of the ball won't crack it. Run two pipes from the back of it near the top (attached to the cement by cement screws) and angled down to the floor to support the block. Then paint the strike zone on the front, about in the middle. Now you can set up your cement block as first base, second or third in their proper positions behind you as pitcher, and work on your pick-off moves by turning and throwing to the base (cement block). Also you will find with working on pitching to a hitter that you are throwing the low strike to your painted target.

BENCH DRILL

These two aids really helped me in my preparation for the season.

How do you teach pitchers a smooth motion?

A pitcher needs to develop a smooth, simple motion. He should stress putting his hip pocket in the hitter's face—especially a sidearm pitcher. Overhand and three-quarter pitchers must emphasize this point also, but not as markedly. The big reason for this is to allow your arm to keep up with your body—otherwise your body will be too quick for your arm, and this will destroy your rhythm and power, as your arm will have to hurry to catch up with your body.

Your fast curve is famous. How do you teach it?

The fingers are moved slightly to the

right on the ball compared to your fast-ball grip, and the motion of the fingers is downward with a lot of pull. There is hardly any strain on the elbow. The thumb does not grip too tightly, as this spoils good wrist action. The thumb can sometimes be flipped from underneath the ball to give you even more spin. The elbow should be slightly bent and closer to the body and head.

The fast curve is effective because of the spin, which appears to be a fast ball on its approach to the hitter, but at the last second breaks very quickly.

There is so little strain to the arm with this pitch that one time when Whitey Ford couldn't throw any effective curves because of arm trouble, he learned this fast-curve pitch and was able to start throwing it right away.

What method do you like to use in teaching pitchers to work on hitters?

I don't feel you can teach eleven pitchers eleven different ways to pitch to any given hitter. A pitcher must challenge a hitter with his best pitch, even if it happens to be in the hitter's best hitting zone. A pitcher must have his best stuff on the ball. Most pitchers' power area is from the waist down. If he pitches here and happens to make a mistake high, he may get away with it; but by the same token if he tries to pitch to a hitter's weakness ("spot pitching") which is the opposite of his own strength, and he loses his best stuff on the ball and makes a mistake with the pitch, he's in real trouble.

What are some of your thoughts on working from the stretch position?

In holding a man on first it is important to have knees bent and to develop quickness to the plate. You must experiment here. [John closed himself up and moved

his front leg way over toward third.] With a man on third, when there is a possibility of a man stealing home or a squeeze play, the pitcher should work from a stretch. The one big advantage of working from a stretch with a runner on third instead of first is that the pitcher can take his time in his delivery to the plate and put something on the ball.

What use do you make of pitching charts?

We can find out several things from them. Generally a hitter will hit ground balls and pop-outs in one direction and line drives and base hits in another. A pitching chart will show this. A pitcher may feel he is getting killed with a certain pitch, and we can go to the charts and see what is really happening with that pitch. We use red for base hits and blue or green for fly-outs and ground balls.

We often hear that a pitcher is a "five- or six-inning pitcher." What would make this pitcher more effective?

Generally, what he needs is another pitch in his repertoire.

How do you work with a pitcher who seems to have lost his stuff for no apparent reason?

A pitcher will lose a pitch when he neglects it. If a pitcher has three or four pitches it would be good for him to spend 50 percent of his time on his best pitch.

What are some of the important mental aspects to pitching?

I like the pitcher who, after losing, doesn't feel that it was tough luck, but goes about finding ways to improve himself. A pitcher gets in a tight situation and makes up his mind he's really going to blow the ball by the hitter; just before his release he really muscles up and he has poor wrist

PITCHING CHART

● – Fast Ball
○ – Curve
✓ – Change
– – Slider
S – Screw Ball
X – Knuckle Ball

Batter

Team _____
Versus _____
At _____
Date _____
Weather _____

Prepared by _____

R _____ H _____ E _____

Pitcher		Fast Ball	Curve	Change	Slider	Screw	Knuckle		Totals
	strikes								
	balls								
	strikes								
	balls								
	strikes								
	balls								
	strikes								
	balls								
	strikes								
	balls								
	strikes								
	balls								

action with a resulting loss of stuff. A catcher who really knows how to handle pitchers will come out to the mound and say, "What's your plan? What do you want to throw?" or possibly, "What are you trying to do?" Even with a young pitcher this catcher is giving him credit for having some sense and building up his confidence. It takes a special temperament to pitch. The two people who look bad if they show emotion on the field are the pitcher and manager.

Concentration must be total. This is where pressure and second-guessing visit the mound, also the worry about how tough this hitter is or the last good hit he got off you. Instead the pitcher should think of the successes he's had against this hitter in similar situations. You have to feel you're the master of the situation.

How often should a pitcher throw?

He should throw some every day, throw enough to get loose but not enough to abuse his arm. You must develop strength in your pitchers' arms, and one of the best ways to do this is by throwing. I feel a pitcher is mentally ready to pitch a game every third day, but physically, over a whole season, this would be hard to maintain.

What do you try to do in your method of coaching and working with pitchers?

First I like to put myself in the pitcher's shoes and ask myself, "How would I pitch with this man's style and stuff?" Then I suggest two or three ideas that might help him. If he tries it out and finds one that helps him, he's happy and adopts it as his own. If I force him to throw one way he will build up resistance to the ideas we'd like to get across.

Some pitching coaches make the error of trying to make all pitchers throw the way they did, even though these pitchers' physical builds and tools are completely different.

In these pictures Dan Spillner shows the importance of using the body and burying that throwing shoulder into the ground. Notice in photo 3 how, as a power pitcher, Spillner has gotten his whole body into the pitch. You could land an airplane on his back—it's so flat.

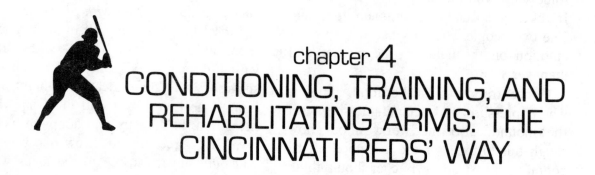

chapter 4
CONDITIONING, TRAINING, AND REHABILITATING ARMS: THE CINCINNATI REDS' WAY

CINCINNATI REDS BASEBALL-STRENGTH TRAINING PROGRAM

Many misconceptions and fallacies have been established concerning weight training principles and objectives. Oftentimes weight training is solely related to the "muscle-bound" individual who is unable to perform naturally. This is not the case with this program and is definitely not the objective of a baseball strength-training program. On the contrary, besides increasing muscular strength and endurance, you will also show increases in joint flexibility and range of motion.

If all other aspects are equal (bodily proportions, neurological efficiency, cardiovascular ability, and skill), the stronger athlete will win. Absolutely nothing can be done to improve either bodily proportions or neurological efficiency; however, we can do something about the other factors. Skill is improved by various drills as well as actually playing the game. Cardiovascular ability is increased through a conditioning program, running, and playing.

Muscular strength can also be increased through a conscientious, properly executed strength-training program.

Strength is important in every sport, including baseball. Although some sports may require higher levels of strength, all baseball activities require some degree of strength. Strength is important to the baseball player for three reasons:

1. Decreases the likelihood of injury.
2. Increases muscular endurance, thus enabling the player to compete for a longer duration without fatigue.
3. Increases the playing lifetime of a player.

Knowing these important and necessary aspects of muscular strength in baseball, you then must decide on the best method of producing the desired results. You actually have four alternatives, listed in order of best productivity:

1. **Nautilus Time Machines**—Best method for producing full-range, high-intensity,

short-duration, strength-training exercise. Nautilus is the only rotary form of automatically varying resistance exercise that includes stretching, pre-stretching, and a full muscular contraction.

2. **Barbell and dumbells**—Limited in full-range exercise but can be beneficial in producing strength increases.
3. **Universal type machines**—Less productive than Nautilus or barbells, but give some results for strength training.
4. **Iso-kinetic (i.e., speed limiting)**—Does not provide the necessary requirements for a full-range exercise program.

Based on a review of the available literature, personal communication with leading sports medicine people, and actual strength-training programs, we have concluded that Nautilus is the best method for developing strength and endurance and for increasing flexibility.

Strength-Training Program

When establishing a strength-training program, you must remember that strength is general, not specific. You should work all joints throughout their complete line of action. It must also be remembered that many injuries are caused by an improper balance between agonist (muscles that move a body part) and antagonist (muscles that oppose that movement). For example, when strengthening the thigh muscles, if we devoted all our time to the quadriceps and ignored the hamstrings, the ultimate result would be numerous injuries to the hamstrings. This would be true for hips, back, shoulders, elbows, and ankles. Keeping these principles in mind and remembering the specific actions and activities necessary in the game of baseball, the following programs should be instituted. (Refer to chart.)

When doing the program, start out with a relatively light weight so that you are sure to execute the exercise in the proper manner. Lifting a weight is not enough, regardless of the amount of weight. How you lift a weight is a factor of far greater importance. You should be able to do at least eight good repetitions. If you cannot do eight, then the weight is too heavy. If you can do twelve or more, then the weight is too light, and you should add another plate or five to ten pounds. The program should stress complete range of motion, attempting to obtain a stretch before executing the movement.

Your off-season conditioning program should start two to five weeks after the season ends. During this period you should concentrate on individual weaknesses and developing strength throughout the entire body. Depending on the type of equipment you are using, you should be working on all twelve muscular areas listed in the chart. Do your strength training on an every-other-day basis, thus allowing your muscles enough time to recover from the work. You should be able to complete the program in approximately one hour or less. Concentrate on form, gradually increasing the resistance as the repetitions become easier. Base your increases on the eight to twelve system as explained above.

Objectives of the Strength-Training Program

1. To increase muscular strength
2. To increase muscular endurance
3. To increase joint flexibility
4. To increase muscular speed

With these objectives in mind, you should practice the following fundamentals when completing EACH repetition:

1. Do all repetitions throughout complete range of motion.
2. Do all repetitions by raising on a 1–2 count and lowering on a 1–2–3–4 count.

Muscle Exercised	Nautilus Time Machines	Barbells and Dumbbells	Universal Gym Station
Lower back, hips, buttocks	Hip and Back Duosymmetric-polycontractile machine	Hip flexor, using high bar	Leg press and hip flexor
Quadriceps	Leg extension	Squats, knee extension	Leg extension station
Hamstring	Leg curl	Squats, knee flexion	Knee station (leg curl)
Calves	Calf raises (Multi-exerciser)	Calf raises—barbell on shoulders	Calf raises, shoulder-press station on shoulders
Upper torso	Super pullover	Bench pullover	High lat. station
Latissimus dorsi	Behind the neck	Bench pullover	High lat. station
Pectoral muscles	Double chest	Bench press	Chest-press station
Deltoids supraspin	Double shoulder	Abduction lift—arm straight at side, lift to shoulder level, and return	Shoulder-press station
Rhomboids rotators	Rowing machine	Rhomboid lift—lying on stomach, arm straight, lift up, and return	Rowing station
Biceps	Biceps curl	Bicep curl	Biceps-curl station
Triceps	Triceps extension	Tricep extension—barbell behind head, arm bent, straighten, and return	Negative dips on dip station
Wrists & forearms	Wrist curl (Multi-exerciser)	Wrist curl	Wrist curl (bicep station), wrist developer station

3. Do all repetitions slowly, making sure to pause briefly at the fully contracted position and at the starting position.
4. Do all repetitions concentrating on form; weight increases will follow accordingly.
5. Do all repetitions in a smooth and controlled manner, without heaving and jerking the weights.
6. Do all repetitions competing against yourself, not other players.

One point that must be stressed is that the strength-training program in no way replaces other phases of your program nor should it be the main ingredient. It is of the utmost importance that you continue your running, throwing, and hitting. However, when done properly, the strength training can be a highly beneficial and rewarding addition to your baseball career.

CINCINNATI REDS OFF-SEASON CONDITIONING PROGRAM

Conditioning for baseball is a twelve-months-a-year job. The purpose of this conditioning program is to develop joint flexibility, muscular endurance, and muscular strength in order to prevent injuries. To perform at his best, a baseball player must be flexible and strong. This program gives you flexibility and cardiorespiratory endurance through stretching, running, and strength training.

Strive to gain a complete range of motion and flexibility in the shoulders, thighs, back, and hips. All players should try to touch their toes without bending their knees. However, if you are unable to do this, you should begin gradually to increase your flexibility and hamstring range until you can touch your toes.

The metal bat he is swinging weighs seven pounds.

Start your swing, launching the bat through as quickly as possible. Take your full swing and follow-through. Hold your follow-through for a split second. Then start your backward swing, and fire the bat as hard and as quickly as you can—like running a movie camera backward. Repeat the drill immediately. Young players start with 20 repetitions. Then add 5 to 10 each time until you reach 100 or more. The key to this drill is to go all out when swinging through and bringing the bat backward. You will be amazed after a month or two of doing this every day by how much faster you become with your hands and bat, making it possible for you to wait longer on a pitch and generate more power.

Stand up straight. Slowly bend at the waist until you feel a stretch, and hold for six seconds. Do not bob or bounce up and down vigorously to force a stretch. Instead, slowly put the muscle on a stretch, and hold for six seconds. Repeat. Stretch every day of the year using this procedure to improve or maintain flexibility in the entire body.

As stated earlier in this chapter, the strength-training program should be done on an every-other-day basis. The only exception would be the first two or three days when you first start to train. Then you should do it three days in a row to overcome some of the stiffness and soreness that you may experience. Each weight-training exercise should be done slowly and in a controlled manner at all times. You should raise the weight to fully contract the muscle on the count of one. Do at least twelve to fifteen repetitions. If you cannot do at least eight good repetitions, then the weight is too heavy. If you can do twelve or more, then it is too light. You need to do only one set of twelve repetitions in good form. Try to increase your range of motion on each exercise, and try to work every muscle through the complete range of contraction. I highly recommend Nautilus weight training if you have access to the machines. If not, I would recommend barbells next, and if not them, then Universal. Your main objective in the off-season should be to work on weaknesses or areas that are limited in strength and/or flexibility.

Flexibility Exercises

1. *Side Straddle Hop* (jumping jacks)— 20 repetitions.
2. *Arm Circles.* Big and little circles, forward and backward—20 repetitions.
3. *Milk the Cow.* With arms at shoulder level, open and close fists—15 repetitions.
4. *Reach for the Sky.* Hold hands apart in front of body and lift slowly overhead; stretch for six seconds; return— 10 repetitions, stretching farther each time.
5. *Upper-Body Twist.* Hold hands apart in front of body; turn trunk to left; hold for six seconds; return; do same to the right—10 repetitions each way.
6. *Side to Side.* Hold hands in front of body; turn trunk to left and hold for six seconds; return; turn to right and hold—10 repetitions each way.
7. *Trunk Bend.* With feet spread apart eighteen to twenty-four inches, legs straight, hands behind back near hips, attempt to put forehead on knee while lifting hands back; hold for six seconds and return; do the same to middle and then right knee—10 repetitions each way.
8. *Windmill.* Extend arms at shoulder level; move feet shoulder width apart; touch right foot with left hand; return; touch left foot with right hand—10 repetitions each foot.
9. *Hamstring Stretch.* Cross one leg in front of the other, feet together; slowly bend over and touch toes; hold for six seconds—10 repetitions with each leg.
10. *Heel Cord Stretch.* Step forward with left foot, heel flat on floor; bend over, touch toes; hold for six seconds; return—10 repetitions with each leg.
11. *Hip Flexor Stretch.* Step forward with one leg, knee bent; with back leg straight, stretch forward and hold for six seconds—repeat 10 times each leg.

Sitting or Reclining Exercises

1. *V-Sit-up.* Lying flat, raise legs and chest at same time while keeping legs straight; hold for six seconds—10 repetitions.
2. *Bent-Knee Sit-up.* Lying on back with knees bent and feet flat on floor, slowly

Members of the North Ridgeville Rangers High School Baseball Team of Ohio demonstrate their flexibility and stretching program. Notice in this sequence how the players stretch all the major muscles in the body before touching the ball: the legs, hamstrings, and calves all the way down to the toes; then the middle body, stomach, arms, shoulders, head, and neck. This is the proper way to prepare for throwing. It increases flexibility and cuts down on the chance of straining a muscle.

These sequences show you only one side of the body. You should reverse and do the other side of your body the same way.

sit-up, and slowly lower yourself back—repeat 30 times (increase to 50).

3. *Single Leg Raises.* Extend legs on floor, and raise arms to shoulder level; raise leg up, knee straight, return—10 repetitions each leg.

4. *Side Leg Raise.* Lie on your side with legs straight; raise top leg and return—10 repetitions while on each side and one leg at a time while on stomach.

5. *Hip Raiser.* Lying on back with knees bent, slowly raise hips toward ceiling, pinching buttocks together; hold for six seconds and return—10 repetitions.

6. *Back-Hip Stretch.* Lying on back with knees bent, grasp knee, and slowly bring up to chest; return—10 repetitions with each leg and both legs.

7. *Leg Raises.* Lying on back with shoulders off floor supported by elbows, lift legs off floor, and hold for six seconds—10 repetitions.

8. *Back Stretch.* Lying on floor with knees bent, flatten out lower back against floor, and pinch buttocks together; hold for six seconds—10 repetitions.

Throwing

Start at a fairly easy and short distance. Then gradually increase your distance until you are at least 60 feet away depending on what position you play. After reaching the desired distance, gradually increase your velocity and duration until you are throwing 150–200 tosses every other day.

Help to make the double play quicker by wearing a wooden glove, which helps you get rid of the ball quicker on the double play.

Running

Although sprinting should be your main concern in running, since most running in baseball is of a short spurt nature, you should also include some long distance running in your off-season program. It is important that you establish an aerobic (oxygen) base, which can only be achieved through a distance of one mile or more. I

(opposite page) This is one of the few drills in baseball that will actually help you to throw harder and give your pitches more velocity. Line up a string of baseballs in short left field just behind shortstop. Pick up a ball, and run back a few steps. Then run forward full speed, and just throw into a backstop. Don't worry about control or anything; just run free and hard, and let the ball fly. Then pick up another ball, and repeat until your arm is tired, at which point you should stop immediately. You may start out with 10 throws and gradually build up to 50 or 60. Notice in photo 15 the major league throwing form on an 11-year-old boy. This is one of the greatest of all throwing drills.

would suggest that you gradually build up to running three to five miles every other day by the end of the off-season. You should time yourself and try to eventually run the mile in under six minutes. But you should also include ten to fifteen sprints of thirty or forty yards apiece to maintain and improve your speed and skill. You can also do pick-ups and run up and down steps.

Lead Baseball Exercises

1. *Forward and Backward Swing.* Stand with feet shoulder width apart; let throwing arm hang loosely with ball in hand; swing ball forward and backward in a pendulum fashion letting ball do the work—15 forward and backward strokes.
2. *Lateral Swing.* Assume same starting position as #1; with ball in throwing hand, swing it from left to right loosely —15 side-to-side strokes with throwing arm.
3. *Circle Swing.* Assume same starting position as #1; with ball in throwing hand, swing it in a clockwise circle—12 circles clockwise and then 12 circles counterclockwise.
4. *Reach for the Sky.* Stand upright with elbow bent at shoulder level and ball in hand; *count 1*—raise ball straight up until bicep touches ear; *count 2*—push higher; *count 3*—higher still; return to starting position, and do not move trunk or feet—10 repetitions.
5. *Rotators Stretch.* Assume same starting position as #4; slowly roll arm forward and then slowly backward as far as possible—go each way 10 times.
6. *Forearm and Wrist Stretch.* Extend arm straight out and support elbow with other hand, with palm facing up and arm stretched out at shoulder level;

bend wrist upward and downward slowly, then rotate wrist right and left—all four movements 10 times.

These exercises can be done with both shoulders. After going through the complete set of exercises, it is suggested that you shake the arm loosely without the ball. If you do not have a lead baseball (which weighs three pounds), you can use a three- or five-pound weight or something that weighs in that range. It is also suggested that everyone do some hanging and stretching daily during the entire off-season. Your goal should be to increase your flexibility in every joint as far as you can.

CINCINNATI REDS REHABILITATIVE THROWING SHOULDER EXERCISES

These exercises are designed to stretch and strengthen the various muscles of the shoulder girdle. In order to throw consistently without injury, the shoulder must be flexible, and *all* muscles must be relatively strong. Doing these exercises will stretch and slightly strengthen those muscles that are most often injured. These exercises should be repeated twice daily until the normal throwing routine is reestablished. They can also be used as a part of the overall conditioning for the throwing shoulder.

1. *Circumduction* (counterclockwise)
   a. Spread feet twenty-four inches apart, bend at the waist.
   b. Allow throwing arm to hang loosely in front of body.
   c. Swing hand, making as large a circle as possible in a counterclockwise direction.
   d. Repeat 10 times.

2. *Circumduction* (clockwise)
   a. Same as above except in a clockwise direction.

3. *Across the Chest Stretch*
   a. Stand with feet apart, arms extended at shoulder level.
   b. Bring throwing arm across chest, keeping arm straight.
   c. With other arm gently push arm down against chest, placing it in a stretch.
   d. Hold this stretch for six seconds.
   e. Repeat 10 times, trying to increase flexibility each time.

4. *Posterior-Anterior Extension* ("sawing wood")
   a. Stand with feet apart and throwing arm bent at side.
   b. Push back with elbow as far as possible and hold for six seconds.
   c. Now bring arm forward and straighten as far as possible.
   d. Hold for six seconds.
   e. Repeat 10 times, trying to increase extension each time.

5. *Supraspinatus Stretch*
   a. Stand with feet apart, arms bent, and hands clasped behind your back, as in an "at ease" position.
   b. Keeping back straight and head back, push elbows and shoulders forward as far as possible.
   c. Hold for six seconds.
   d. Repeat 10 times.

6. *Shoulder Shrug*
   a. Stand with feet apart, arms straight at side.
   b. Raise shoulders up as far as possible.
   c. Hold for six seconds.
   d. Repeat 10 times.

7. *Shaking and Hanging*
   a. Let arms hang loosely and shake freely.
   b. Hang with both arms; then let go and hang with one arm.

chapter 5
RETURN TO THROWING AFTER AN INJURY

INTRODUCTION

The following program is meant to educate the athlete about the proper way to return to throwing after injury to the shoulder, arm, elbow, forearm, or wrist. It is meant to provide a method for progressive return to full activity, emphasizing good form, proper warm-up, strength and flexibility, and the proper use of heat and cold. It is extremely important that the athlete use pain as a guide in performing all activities. For example, if pain is produced in the back, shoulder, or elbow during any phase of the throwing motion, that pain can act much like the recoil of a gun —the stronger it is the greater the recoil, the less the accuracy. The throwing motion may then be thrown off or altered, and as a result, pain is produced in other parts of the extremity.

Section 1: USE OF HEAT AND COLD

I. Heat

Use a form of *moist* heat.
> *Examples:*
> shower
> whirlpool
> hot towels
> hydrocollator pack

The heat should be applied for approximately 20 minutes. *Do not* follow with analgesic balms of any type.

II. Cold

Use for approximately 20 minutes.
> *Examples:*
> ice packs
> ice towels (wet towels rolled in crushed ice)
> ice soak (¼ ice, ¾ cold water; wrap

arm with ice, etc., to help accustom extremity to temperature).

Section 2: WARM-UP FOR THE THROWING ARM

Use a 3- to 5-pound dumbbell, weight, or weighted ball for the following exercises.

I. Forward and Backward Swing

Starting Position: Stand with feet about two feet apart, trunk bent forward, and arms (L or R) hanging loosely with weight in hand.

Action: Swing weight forward and backward like a pendulum. The swing is from the shoulder, the weight doing the work. *Do not* swing with the muscles or from the elbow.

Forward and Backward Swing

II. Lateral Swing

Starting Position: Same as in exercise I.

Action: With weight in right hand, swing weight pendulumlike from left to right, 15 to 20 times. If holding weight in left hand, begin swing from right to left.

Lateral Swing

III. Circle Swing

Starting Position: Same as in exercises I and II.

Action: Swing weight in a clockwise direction making a circle about two feet in diameter depending upon length of arm. Continue with 15 circles, and then make 15 circles counterclockwise. Repeat with other arm.

IV. Up-Stretch

Starting Position: Stand upright. Bend elbow 90° and bring to shoulder level. Hold weight in hand up to perpendicular position.

Action: Raise weight straight upward until the biceps touches ear to count of one. Push a little higher to the limits to count of three. Relax to starting position. Repeat 10 times. Trunk remains erect and facing forward throughout exercise.

Circle Swing. In this exercise we like to use an 8 to 10 pound metal ball, as you can see in sequence. (We feel this really loosens up the arm and shoulder muscles, especially in a big pitcher.)

Up-Stretch

V. Arm Rotator

Starting Position: Stand upright. With weight in hand, bend elbow and bring elbow to shoulder level. Forearm should be up and perpendicular to elbow.

Action: Move weight slowly forward to shoulder level position with weight downward. Wrist, weight, and elbow are now at shoulder level. Raise weight slowly upward, keeping elbow at shoulder and continue moving weight up and back as far as possible without bending body. Continue this forward and backward motion of weight 10 times. Repeat with opposite arm.

VI. Forearm Stretching and Strengthening

Starting Position: Place right wrist under and back of left elbow. Keep left elbow about shoulder level and arm stretched out in front. Hold weight in palm of hand (palm should be facing up.)

Action: Bend left wrist upward and downward. Then slowly rotate arm palm down as you repeat the up and down motion. Repeat this 10 times. Repeat with the right arm.

Arm Rotator

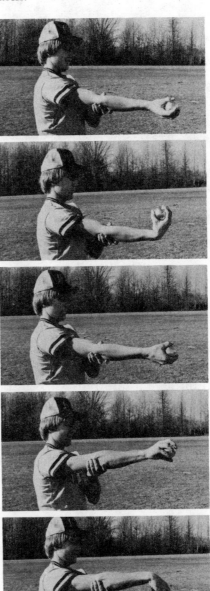

Forearm Stretching and Strengthening

VII. Hang from Bar

Hang from a chin-up bar or from any overhead bar that is strong enough to support your weight. *Do not hang for more than 30 seconds at a time*. Repeat 3 times.

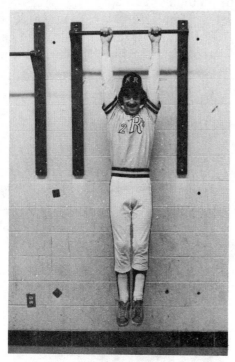

Hang from Bar

Section 3: PROGRESSIVE RETURN TO THROWING AFTER INJURY

Purpose: To permit a full return to throwing by stretching and strengthening the arm through a throwing workout of progressive intensity and duration.

Always begin the workout with a proper warm-up. This is an absolute must! Moist heat, such as steam packs, hot towels, or a shower to the shoulder, neck, and arm muscles may be beneficial. The benefit from analgesics is highly questionable: The massaging during application provides the value. After heat do the previously described warm-up exercises.

Type I: (primarily for the thrower with chronic, severe arm pain)

1. Measure out and mark a line: 90 feet long, first marker at 20 feet from thrower, and every 10 feet thereafter place another marker.

2. Depending upon your symptoms and any specific instructions given by the trainer, begin by throwing the ball at a specified marker. You may place a target, such as a basket etc., out at the marker to receive the ball. Work for 5-20 minutes, throwing a *maximum* of 15 pitches with a ball. Note both the time and number of throws during that time on the record sheet. You may choose to only go through the motion for a while as a prethrowing warm-up. Concentrate on form!!

3. Your throwing workout will be limited by one of three factors:
   a. The 20 minute maximum time is up.
   b. The maximum number of pitches allowed is reached.

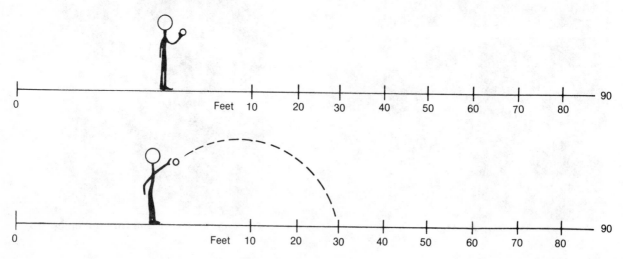

c. There is pain on the throwing motion. By throwing into increasing pain, you may cause a "recoil effect" throwing your delivery off and causing more problems.

4. After workout, pack the shoulder, arm, and elbow in ice for 20 minutes.

To Increase the Workout

1. By increasing the distance (20 feet to 30 feet to 40 feet . . . to 90 feet), *you are increasing the intensity of the exercise* (similar to increasing the amount of weights you are lifting). As with weights, it is important NOT to jump from 20 to 40 to 60, etc. Limit your increases to 10 feet at a time.
2. By increasing the maximum number of pitches.
   Use a "5 by 5 rule":
   Add 5 more pitches to the workout PLUS 5 more minutes.
   An example of a workout and how to use the workout record sheet is attached.

Remember:

1. Proper warm-up precedes any throwing.
2. Moist heat can be used before workout.
3. Progressive workout, including weight training.
4. Ice after workout.

Type II: (primarily for the thrower with the less painful but limiting injury who needs to slowly get back into shape.)

Each *Step* states its basic requirements and conditions for proceeding on to the next *Step*. It may take you several days to fulfill those requirements. *DO NOT RUSH OR PUSH BEYOND THE LIMITS OF PAIN.* Record on the record sheets where you are at all times.

Step 1: Long, easy throws from deepest portion of the outfield, with the ball just barely getting back to fungo hitter. To be performed for 30 minutes on two consecutive days.
Then REST the arm for one day.

Step 2: Stronger throws from the mid-outfield, getting ball back on 5 to 6 bounces. To be performed for 30 minutes on two consecutive days.
Then REST for a day.

Step 3: Strong, crisp throws with a relatively straight trajectory from the short outfield, on one bounce back to fungo hitter. Again, for 30 minutes on two consecutive days.
Then REST for a day.

Step 4: Return to the mound or other normal position for usual activities.

A Sample Workout—Type I

Day	Distance (feet)	Time Spent (minutes)	Number of Throws	Comments
1st	20	5		
2nd		10		some soreness
3rd		10		no pain
4th		15		
5th		20		feels good
6th	30	5		feels good- no soreness
7th		10		
8th		15		some soreness
9th		15		O.K.
10th		20		
11th	40	5		

chapter 6
THE MAJOR LEAGUE WAY TO MAINTAIN A BASEBALL FIELD

The master craftsman of baseball fields, Marshall Bossard.

How important is a major league grounds keeper? Many of you remember years ago when Bill Mazeroski of the Pirates hit his historical and tremendously exciting home-run in the World Series against the Yankee's. But how many of you remember that the hitter before hit a routine ground ball to Tony Kubek, which hit on the infield at Forbes Field (purposely kept rock hard because the Pirates had a lot of line-drive and infield hitters) and took a bad hop, catching Kubek in the Adam's apple. If this hadn't happened, Mazeroski wouldn't have even come to bat.

Since the condition of the baseball field is this important on the major league level, you certainly can improve your baseball-playing ability by having your field in major league shape, which can be done with hard work and some real knowledge. So I went to the dean of major league grounds keepers, Marshall Bossard of the Cleveland Indians. Marshall along with his family have made grounds keeping a profession spanning three generations, and they have invented some tools that can help bring your field up to major league quality if they are used properly.

"Marshall, your field year in and year out is one of the most beautiful ball parks in the country. Infielders like Craig Nettles say your infield is one of the finest to play on in the world, which is the real measure of a park. How do you accomplish this?"

"You have to give it loving care and be on it at all times. You can never get behind or you're lost."

With these conscientious words he explains the grounds-keeping duties that have been an integral part of his life for more than forty years.

"As soon as the team leaves on the road, you have to jump on whatever weak spots you expect. Generally, you can tell what is going to come up by looking at the field and just through experience." If experience is the key to keeping a field in major league shape, Bossard is well qualified.

His eighty-eight-year-old father Emil assumed the grounds-keeping chores for the Yankees' St. Paul, Minnesota, farm club back in 1920. After turning down two previous offers, the elder Bossard accepted the invitation of then tribe owner Alva Bradley to ready the Cleveland field within ninety days. Packing up his rake and family, Emil journeyed to Cleveland to become head grounds keeper in 1935.

"Harold came to Cleveland with my dad, but I decided to stay in St. Paul for another year of experience," explained Marshall, the middle of three Bossard brothers. "I joined my older brother Harold and my father in 1936 and have been in Cleveland ever since.

"After about three or four years we decided to make this our life. Whereas we had originally considered it a job, we now thought that we should make grounds keeping our profession."

And after forty-three years on the Cleve-

Major league ballyard, Cleveland Municipal Stadium.

land diamond, Marshall is undoubtedly the elder statesman of major league grounds keepers. Both his father Emil and brother Harold have retired, and now the sixty-three-year-old Bossard offers the most respected advice of any big league park caretaker. He serves as a consultant on field care for baseball people worldwide.

"You have to be tuned in to your ball players. It's like you're one of them. If there is any way you can help out the ball players on your club, then you go out of your way to do it. I help the players in whatever way I can with the field. Since the Indians are running a lot more this year, I make the base paths fast. The area around first base is a little harder this year so that they can get a good jump."

Yet, the strengths and weaknesses of the Indians' opponents often dictate the way Marshall will prepare the field:

"If I feel that against a certain team we may be in several bunting situations, then I'll build up the foul lines a little so the balls stay fair. When the tribe goes up against a running ball club, I drag the dirt around first base a little more and loosen it up so they don't get as good a start."

To Marshall, infield preparation is virtually a science. With good sunshine and eighty-five-degree temperatures, he will sprinkle the infield dirt an average of one and one-half to two hours a day. In moist weather the infield requires less water. (Both of these should be done several hours before game time.)

Infielders like the dirt around their position to be like a cushion underneath and dry on top. When players come here, they know that the ball will hop true and that there won't be any surprises. The infield grass is watered for fifteen minutes each day, and the inner and outer edges are manicured regularly. The worn-out grass around the pitcher's mound and in front of

home plate is replaced with sod during each road trip, and the field dimensions are checked religiously.

Yet probably more important than the infield is the pitcher's mound, a fifteen-inch hill upon which Marshall wages a constant battle against every hurler's own personal grounds-keeping touches. The mound has to be built up after almost every game. With pitchers digging in next to the rubber and digging even deeper into the mound where they follow through, we have to repack the mound with mud, clay, and dirt after almost every game.

And there were times when the Bossards rebuilt practically the entire mound overnight. "Back in the late thirties Johnny Allen, who was a submarine pitcher, liked the mound built at twelve inches rather than the regulation fifteen. When he got through pitching one day at twelve inches, we'd have to rebuild the entire mound overnight so that it was back to fifteen inches for Bob Feller the next day. Because of Feller's fastball, he liked to come off a mountain of a mound."

As for the grass, Marshall puts the same time and care into his three-and-a-half-acre plot that the average homeowner on a much smaller scale puts into his own backyard.

"I fertilize the grass once every month and water it depending on the weather conditions. My routine is not much different from anyone else's," conceded Bossard. Though the routine may not differ, the quantity of supplies certainly does. The Bossard crew spreads an average of five tons of fertilizer on the field each year, comparable to about 500 of the commercial bags one would find in his neighborhood nursery.

"Marshall, how would you start on an infield in poor condition, a pasture, or a new field?"

"First I believe I would Roto-Till the skinned part of the infield three inches deep and then bring in three loads of topsoil (or peat), one load of clay, and one load of *completely clean* sand and then mix them together. This mix will give you a good infield in most parts of the country." All these added ingredients must be free of rocks and pebbles or you and the team have to take them out yourself. To make sure his sand is clean, Marshall has devised an excellent tool for screening it. He uses very fine mesh screen (about one-eighth-inch square) stretched between two boards to sift all the sand through. (Be sure your sand is dry before sifting it.)

much better drainage and a chance to play with good footing on the field. The big secret in being able to play is to have the *sand come to the top after a rain.*"

"I notice in Cleveland your ground crew spends a tremendous amount of time dragging the field, and they always do it by hand with a special drag. Why?"

"First, the drag was originated by my dad, and it is unique. It is made up of sixteen penny nails and 2x4s. He invented the idea of having a drag that would go over each piece of dirt. When dragging, don't drag as much in a player's position. Drag between where infielders play. In an emergency you may put big weights and rocks

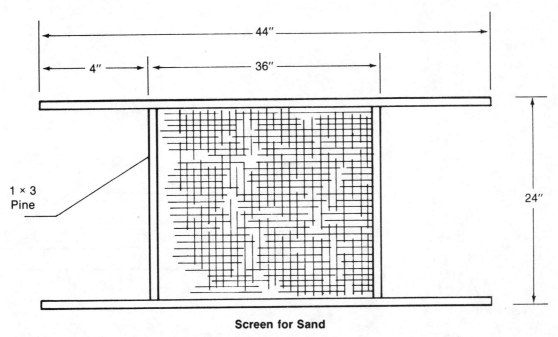

Screen for Sand

"After you've mixed this in the dirt part of your infield (preferably in the fall so that the winter will set it for you), then roll it, and if possible add a half inch of sand for a top dressing over the entire dirt part of your infield. Then water the sand so the water soaks in. Also work the sand into the clay and topsoil. The reason for this is that when the rains come, the sand will work its way to the top giving you

on the drags to help them dig in. A real key to dragging a day before a game is to go over all parts of the skinned infield by hand and drag in both directions. Drag the short way back and forth. Also, drag the long way, starting at the back. Vary which way you start, first short or long.

"Another drag we use that my dad invented is a *smoothing drag* to be used after the nail drag. Walk backwards with this

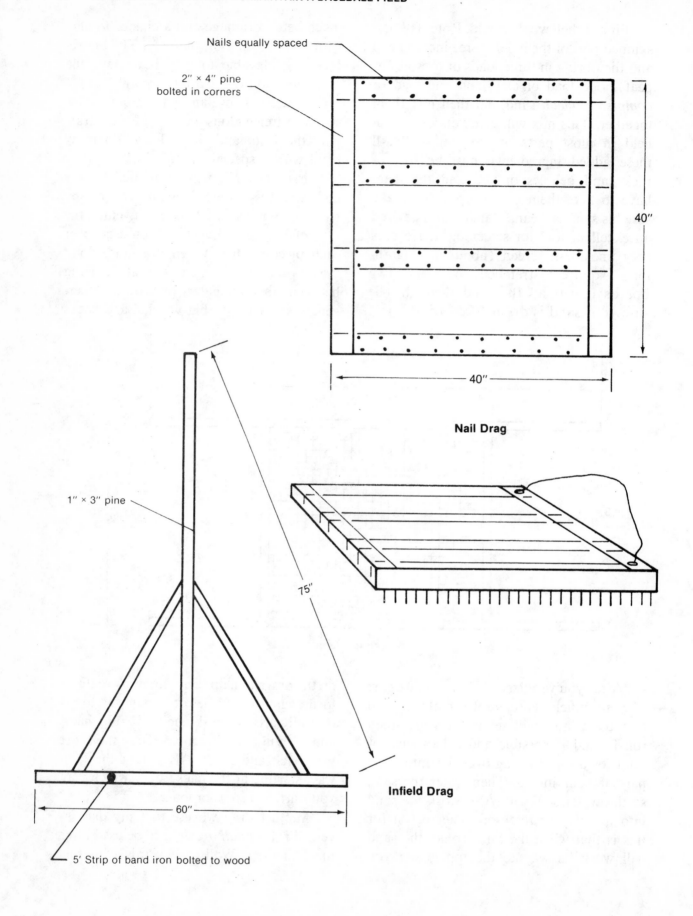

Nails equally spaced

2″ × 4″ pine
bolted in corners

40″

40″

Nail Drag

1″ × 3″ pine

75″

60″

Infield Drag

5′ Strip of band iron bolted to wood

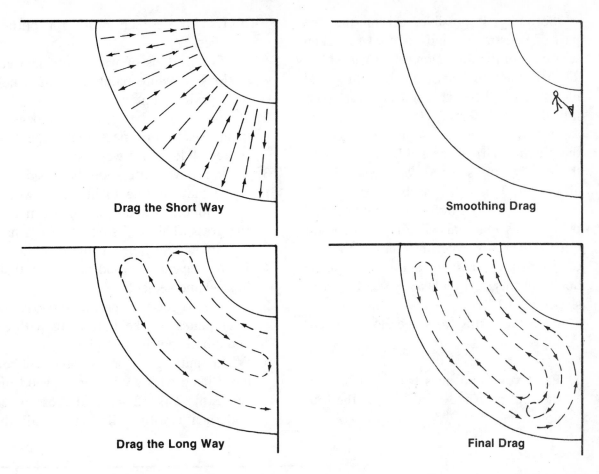

Drag the Short Way

Smoothing Drag

Drag the Long Way

Final Drag

smoothing drag, holding it belt high. It will fill holes and level, besides gathering any pebbles. When using this drag start leveling from the back of the infield. Wherever you start from is where you finish."

"How do you repair the mound and home plate area after a game?"

"Get an old-fashioned bathtub, put three or four bags of clay in the tub. Then mix this clay like cement, making it sticky. The clay should stick to your hands. Then pack the clay together into balls the size of softballs. Put them out in the sun to dry, and then store them. When you get a hole in front of the mound, you dig out in front of the rubber and the front of the mound. Usually then you will replace this area with about twelve clay balls and tamp down which will give your pitchers a solid base. If you want the clay softer, water with a *sprinkling can.* At home plate do the same

with the holes and use some topsoil with your clay balls. Try to put the clay in early in the morning or the day before a game.

"Here are some other tips while doing this at home plate. Scrape the loose clay, and wet home plate that night; then put in *dry* clay the next morning. Fix mound and home plate *every day.* Otherwise you have to go deeper and deeper every time you fix it."

"What are some of your ideas about trying to get a baseball field playable after a rain?"

"Don't ever pour gasoline on the dirt and light it. It may make the field playable that day, but in the process you are destroying the texture of the soil. You *destroy the dirt; it actually dies.* The dirt becomes powdery and useless after the intense heat. (The texture of your dirt is vital to a good field.)

"Secondly, if possible, get on the dirt part of your infield and just make chicken scratches in the dirt. *Don't rake very deep.* Then if the sun comes out and the wind blows you will be surprised how fast your infield will dry out. (Of course, sweep away any puddles or standing water off the playing part of the field.) If you have the money, buy some sacks of *Speedi Dry* absorbent. This will absorb water and dry out the skinned part of your infield beyond belief. This material will dry up puddles, but the secret is to let it come off the end of your shovel and *put it on very lightly; don't put this stuff on heavily.* (It is expensive though.)"

Some other tips from the Bossards' encyclopedia:

1. Paint your foul lines from first base to the foul pole and third base to the foul pole.

   a. Use a 3½-inch brush for outfield lines.
   b. Two gallons of water with five gallons of white paint. Use latex field marking paint, white.

2. If you use peg bases, use four pegs on each base. Four pegs make the base more solid; then it won't shift.

3. If you have hitters on both sides of home plate hitting to infielders with a grass infield, spread an old fish net on the grass. This will stop you from having divots and holes in the infield.

4. If you have hollywood bases, set them in steel and cement.

5. To make a good tamper, weld two round steel plates on the bottom of a three-and-a-half-foot hollow pipe.

6. When putting in a pitching rubber, build it up with six inches of wood underneath. Take 2x4s, and cross block underneath with nails. Then nail the

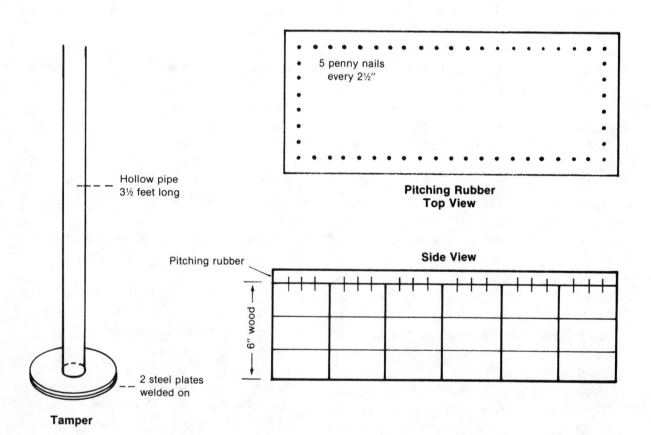

Hollow pipe 3½ feet long

2 steel plates welded on

Tamper

5 penny nails every 2½"

**Pitching Rubber
Top View**

Side View

Pitching rubber

6" wood

**Home Plate
Top View**

rubber to this block of wood with five-penny nails every two and a half inches. Nail whole rubber. This will make a level solid pitching rubber that won't allow any dirt to work its way under.

7. Do the same with home plate putting the nails all the way around the black part of the plate.

You have now got the inside view and shared thinking of a master craftsman and nothing can compete with the experience and knowledge of Marshall Bossard. The fatherly care and concern he has for his field gives the name Head Major League Grounds Keeper a whole new meaning.

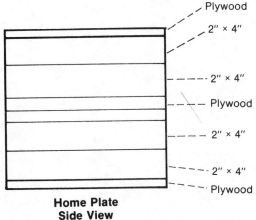

Plywood

2" × 4"

2" × 4"

Plywood

2" × 4"

2" × 4"
Plywood

**Home Plate
Side View**

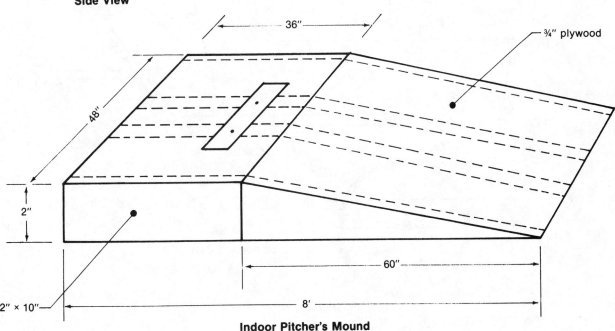

36"

¾" plywood

48"

2"

2" × 10"

60"

8'

Indoor Pitcher's Mound

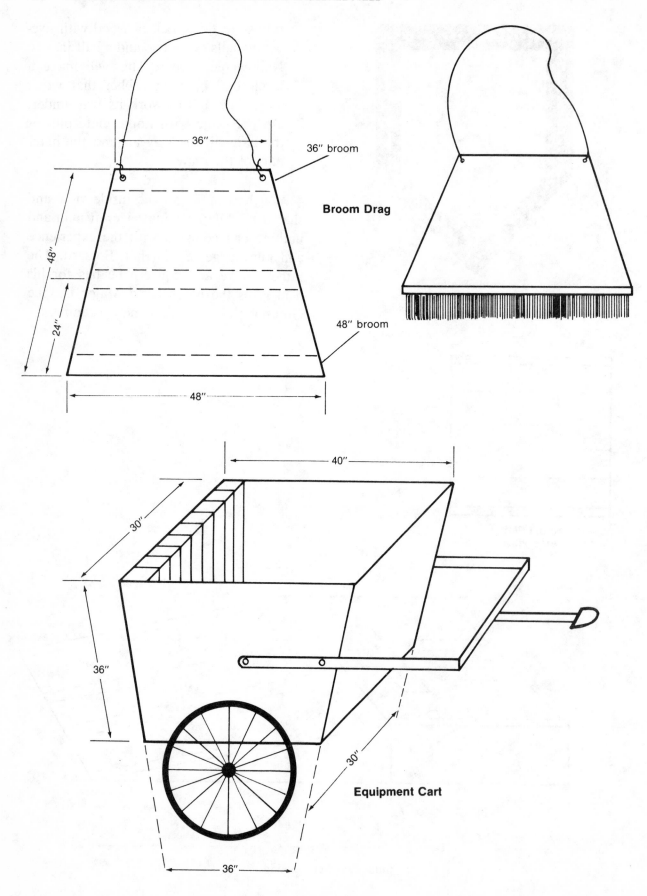

36"

36" broom

Broom Drag

48"

24"

48" broom

48"

40"

30"

36"

30"

36"

Equipment Cart

chapter 7
MECHANICS OF HITTING

Bobby Bonds demonstrates one of the most important fundamentals of hitting in this fantastic photo: the ability to keep your eye on the ball all the way to the bat and also to keep your head still. Notice that even when his bat is shattering in his hands, he is still concentrating so completely on trying to see the ball hit the bat; nothing else matters. All great hitters have this ability.

When you are learning to hit, it is helpful to keep in mind the woodchopper's action in attacking a tree. The woodchopper is relaxed but determined when he approaches the tree, and he swings his axe easily and naturally. He doesn't worry about what the tree will do to him. The tree is always there, and he is always confident that he will hit it.

Now replace the axe with a bat and you will have the makings of a sound baseball swing!

A good swing requires smoothness, rhythm, timing, and balance. Some hitters come by these things naturally, thanks to superior reflexes and timing. Most hitters, however, have to be taught.

Perhaps the two essentials are watching the ball right through to contact with the bat, and keeping a still head. The head is particularly important in baseball, just as it is in nearly every other sport.

The diver depends upon his head to lead the way and guide his body through the air. He knows that any move of his head will automatically shift his body. The golfer knows that a still head is the prime requisite of a good swing. The placement kicker glues his eyes on the ball and holds his head steady throughout the kick—just as the batter watches the ball until it meets his bat.

The hitter who keeps his head still— who doesn't pull it away from the pitch or move it toward the pitcher or bob it up and down—is very likely to have a smooth and rhythmical swing. Chances are, too, that he won't overstride. He'll keep his back foot securely anchored to the ground, and he'll move his hips out of the way to let the bat come around. He will avoid dipping his hips or his body, thus lowering his center of gravity and permitting the ball to slide over his bat. He'll meet the ball out in front squarely and powerfully with the fat end of the bat.

FUNDAMENTALS OF GOOD FORM

Stance

The hitter should assume a natural stance—that is, the position natural for him, the position that gives him the most comfort. It is all right to copy someone else's style, as long as it is right for the particular hitter. Many boys will adopt a style that is wrong for them, or experiment with too many positions. This leads to bad hitting habits and will prevent them from swinging easily and naturally.

Proper stance should allow complete coverage of the plate. It should be close enough to the plate to cover the outside corner, and just far enough away from the inside corner to prevent being handcuffed by the inside strike (being jammed or hit on the fists). The width of the stance usually is based on the height of the player and the type of hitter he is. The power hit-

ter usually uses a wide stance, the hand hitter a narrow one. Feet should be parallel, or nearly so, and comfortably apart; shoulders and hips level, body fairly erect, knees slightly flexed, and weight evenly distributed and inclined slightly forward on the toes. Some hitters will vary their stance against certain pitchers—moving up in the box against breaking-ball pitchers and deeper in the box against fast ballers. The deeper you stand in the box, the more time you have to look the pitch over.

Bat Position

The bat should be held diagonally (neither too vertically nor too horizontally). It should be held completely still, away from the body and as high as is comfortably possible in readiness to lash out instantly at the pitch. There are both advantages and disadvantages to holding the bat either horizontally or vertically. Babe Ruth held his bat in a vertical position, and for that reason was a low-ball hitter. The average batter couldn't possibly hit a high pitch with his bat pointed toward the heavens. Tris Speaker held his bat very flat at shoulder level and looked at the pitcher from over his elbow. As a result he was a good high-ball hitter.

The so-called "level" swing is not always ideal, either. It must originate at the shoulders; it's only from these that the bat can be swung without dipping or sliding, on a plane actually parallel with the ground. But, ironically, a pitch shoulder-high isn't in the strike zone.

At every other position, above and below the shoulder, the ball must be hit with the bat at an angle to the ground. Of course, it's possible to try to level the swing by dropping the hips, pulling back or otherwise shifting the body. On a low pitch it is possible to bend the back knee and lower the back leg which will give a driving swing on the low pitches. But these movements entail a shifting of the head, a lowering of the center of gravity, and other form faults that impair power and timing. After a hitter has taken his stance, feels comfortable and has his bat back and wrists cocked, he will be looking at the pitcher over his front shoulder with his body generally parallel to the expected flight of the ball.

The point is that each batter should find his own natural swing. He can do this by running a swing in reverse (like running a motion picture backward). He reaches out with his bat in front of him as far as

Willie Stargell glides into the pitch and really attacks the ball. Willie is a very disciplined hitter. Notice in the middle photos how he is exploding into the ball.

possible and then brings it back and up over his shoulder quickly to whatever position it naturally goes.

The Stride

A split second before or just as the pitcher delivers the ball, the batter slides his front foot forward. If he keeps his head still, he won't be able to stride too far. (Have someone hold the batter's head and then ask him to stride; the farthest he'll be able to move his foot is about twelve inches, and there his foot will be braced.)

The batter must begin to rotate his body as he starts to bring the bat forward. He must pivot on the front foot during his swing to further open his hips. If he doesn't pivot, he'll lock his hips and cramp his follow-through. However, he must be careful not to rotate or open up before the pitch, as this will kill all his power.

With his hips out of the way, his arms are completely free to swing the bat in a wide arc. It's at the peak of this arc that the ball is hit. By this time his body is almost, but not quite, squarely facing the pitcher. Contact is established off a braced straight front leg, while the back leg is bent at the knee and the weight is up on the toes. The body power flows behind the bat, and the batter actually hits the ball as much as a foot in front of his body, rather than reaching out across the plate or pulling away. The batter who connects out in front actually can see the ball-bat contact. The bat may be in one of three different positions when it meets the ball: (1) way out in front of the body in order to pull, (2) half-way out in front to hit up the middle, or (3) barely in front to hit to right field (right-handed hitter).

Hands

The wrists uncock as the ball is hit, imparting a final flick to the bat that produces extra power. Both arms should be straight, reaching as far out as they comfortably can to provide the wide arc that increases power. In the follow-through, the right wrist rolls over the left (for right-handed hitter). The head remains still. This helps keep the back foot anchored until the follow-through finally brings that foot up on the toe or just slightly off the ground.

Summing Up

The hitting action may be summarized as follows: Assume a comfortable, well-balanced, erect stance, holding the bat diagonally and as high as you comfortably can. While keeping your head perfectly still, take a controlled stride into the pitch and bring the bat forward.

At the same time, take your hips out of the way by turning your body and pivoting on your front foot. Hit off a braced front leg, establishing contact at least a foot in front of your body where you can see the ball. Keep your arms away from your body so that the bat can describe a full arc. Guide the bat with your front arm and apply the power with a bent back arm, which straightens out with the uncocking of the wrists. Make the swing one smooth, rhythmical movement. And remember, you can't be thinking of all these things while you're doing them. Everything must be made automatic by constant practice.

READING A PITCHER

The analysis of the pitcher should begin in the on-deck circle. The hitter should first study the pitcher's fast ball. If possible, he should try to detect how he throws it, how it moves, where it is usually thrown, when it's thrown—anything that can help him read and time the pitch. Note whether the pitcher does anything different on his curve: if he keeps his hands together higher over his head, if he executes a different kind of leg kick, if he fingers the ball differently, and so on. See whether he winds up differently when he throws a change-up, and if he shows the batter the white of the ball at any time.

A close study of the pitcher on the rubber can reveal the following: (1) what type of pitch he will throw, (2) if he takes something off the pitch to get it over when behind, (3) if he relies on a fast ball or curve whenever he gets in a hole, (4) if he's high-ball or low-ball pitcher, (5) if he pitches sidearm or straight overhand, (6) which way his pitches break, (7) if he pitches a left-hand hitter differently from a righty, (8) if he throws as well from a stretch position, and (9) if he observes a definite pitching pattern, such as always trying to get the first pitch over, what kind of pitch he uses to get it over, how he moves the ball around, what he throws in a jam, etc.

The infielders and outfielders also may give away the pitch by certain actions, such as moving a step or two to the power field on a curve ball, cheating a step or two to the opposite field on a fast ball, or leaving gaps in certain areas. Since the catcher also may shift his target on certain pitches, he, too, should be studied.

PSYCHOLOGY OF HITTING

Branch Rickey once said, "The biggest difference between major and minor leaguers is the hitter's attitude when he steps into the box and when the pitch is on its way. The hitter must have a positive approach: 'I'm going to hit the pitch.' He must be ready and set, with his wrists cocked to swing, and he should start forward with the pitch. If the pitch is out of line, he should ease off and let it go. The wrong approach is: 'If it is in there, I'll hit it.' The hitter should never assume a defeatist attitude."

The hitter should have confidence in his ability to meet any situation, no matter how tough it is, and he should dare the pitcher to get one past him. Determination can compensate for batting flaws or a general lack of ability. Whenever the hitter has two strikes on him, he must guard the plate. The plate and his strike zone immediately enlarge, and he should swing at anything that is close, choking up on the bat and shortening his swing. When fooled by a curve ball with less than two strikes on him, the batter should take the pitch; the percentages show that if he swings, he'll hit a weak grounder or pop-up. He should try to pick up the spin of the ball as the pitcher releases it. An overspin (like a top) means a curve, and a reverse spin means a fast ball.

In practice you can have the hitter put a patch over one eye and then over the other to determine which one is focusing for him. After affixing the patch, the hitter should stand at the plate, take the pitches, and follow the ball all the way into the catcher's mitt, always studying the spin of the ball.

The good hitter doesn't swing at bad pitches. He makes the pitcher come into the strike zone. And he is always looking for the fast ball. If he's ready for the fast ball he can adjust his timing for the slower curve and change-ups, but if he starts out by looking for the curve, he'll never be able to get around in time to hit the fast ball.

HITTING FAULTS

Several of the more serious hitting faults include:

Dipping

The batter bends his knees, pulls his hips back, and then waves at the ball as it goes by. By taking his body out of the swing, he loses power. The hitter must stand erect. A little flex at the knees is all right, but it must be only a little. When you go down any deeper, you lower your head.

Overstriding

It is not necessary to take a long stride in order to hit a long ball. In fact, the contrary is true. The long stride locks the hips and prevents the body turn. This, in turn, locks the arms. The bat, instead of swinging in an arc, is actually dragged forward.

The wrist snap thus becomes minimal, and the sliding bat will usually go under the ball and produce a pop-up. Even though the hitter may be braced against his front leg, he has completely locked up his power.

To go back to the analogy we began with: Nobody ever swung an axe at a tree by pulling back away from it or by sliding his body beyond the tree and dragging the axe after it.

Hitching

Obviously, any jerk of the hands up or down kills proper timing. It spoils the smoothness and rhythm of the hitting action and forces the batter to rush his swing in order to meet the ball. Furthermore, it forces the batter to start his forward swing from below his shoulders or from his waist, instead of from above the shoulders. This means he must hit up at the ball. Remember that tree: Nobody moves his hands up and down before swinging the axe.

FILMING HITTERS

There's an old saying that a camel believes he's the most beautiful creature in the animal kingdom because he can't see the humps on his back. The same applies to hitters.

Movies can be a big help in this respect. They enable both the coach and the hitter to see exactly what the hitter is doing. The hitter should be filmed during both a hot streak and a dry spell so he and his coach can see just what the hitter was doing differently at these times.

TIPS FROM THE GREAT

Wally Moses, major league batting coach, is convinced that preparation at the plate is one of the most important aspects of hitting. Many hitters start their hands back slowly before the pitch is delivered. Al Kaline bends his knees and plants his weight firmly on both feet. Some hitters like to close their stance by moving their back foot away from the plate. With just a very slight movement, this puts them into excellent position to attack the ball.

Here are Moses' ideas on hitting.

The stride must be easy and slow. The best time to start it is just as the pitcher is about to release the ball. Then with an easy stride, you can actually time the ball. If it's a fast ball, all you have to do is accelerate your stride. The hitter who steps right out with a fast stride won't be able to hit with power, as he commits himself too soon. It's not really important where the batter strides so long as his stride is easy and is started as the pitcher reaches his release point. The bat must have some momentum before or as the swing is started.

The bottom hand is the quick working hand, and the hitter should let it open his shoulder and hip. But he shouldn't open up too soon, unless he wants to go to the opposite field. The shoulder and hip should be kept in until the last split second.

When the swing reaches his belt buckle, the hitter should really accelerate forward.

He should wield the bat with force, getting power behind his swing and driving his back leg and body hard against his front leg. This makes for a good driving stroke.

When a batter is learning to hit the curve, he should try to pick up the rotation of the ball soon after the pitcher releases it and determine where it will break; that's the point on which to concentrate the swing.

George Foster is one of the best hitters in baseball and one of the strongest. He can swing a 40- to 42-ounce bat and get it around on really fast pitches. He can wait until the last second and seemingly hit the ball out of the catcher's mitt.

In this sequence notice how he bends his back leg to get himself in position to go down, get the pitch, and hit it with authority.

Remember this about hitting practice: Nobody can swing more than thirty or forty times with complete concentration. Ten minutes of hitting is about the limit for maximum concentration and effort.

A good hitter must have a fast bat. The bat should be gripped with the fingers, not jammed into the palms. This grip gives the batter much better snap and speed.

All weight should be on the back foot so the hitter can throw body and bat at the ball (as an infielder does when he throws the ball). It is extremely important for a hitter to keep his weight on his back foot so he doesn't commit his weight forward too soon and lose his power. This also helps to keep the head back and still. (A batter I know recently changed his batting stance by closing it more and raising the heel of his front foot to help keep his weight on the back foot. He raised his batting average fifty points.)

A key point in hitting is this: The hitter must be able to generate power with his *arms fully extended*.

The batter should maintain a positive attitude about hitting. He should think about the successes he's had in the past. He should be confident. He should look for pitchers' mistakes and know just how he'll handle them when they come.

Ted Williams, a keen student of hitting, has this advice for batters:

Concerning the alignment of wrists and knuckles on the bat: A turn of your top hand either clockwise or counterclockwise can help you on high and low pitches. A clockwise turn of the top hand (for a right-handed batter) facilitates the down-swing, making it easier to hit a high pitch. A counterclockwise turn of the top hand helps the hitter uppercut the low pitch.

On your first trip to the plate, don't swing at the first pitch. And if that first one is a ball, take another pitch. This gives you the best chance to find out as much as you can about the pitcher. Later on in the game you can swing at any pitch that you have timed.

When you bring the bat back at the start of the swing, you can get all the momentum you need by drawing your hands back along the plane of the swing at the same time you start your stride.

Practice hitting to develop a fast bat. Speed up your stroke from the start to the point of contact with the ball.

Here are the ideas on hitting emphasized by two major league teams:

The Houston Astros are taught that to be a successful hitter, you must learn to wait for the ball. Draw your hands back slowly as you stride into the ball so that you are prevented from lunging at it.

Follow the ball closely until it actually contacts the bat.

Try to wait until the last split second before committing yourself to a pitch.

One of the most crucial aspects of hitting is bat speed. If you have a good fast swing, you should be a good hitter. A speedy bat enables you to: pull the good fast ball; wait longer to start your swing and thus avoid swinging at as many bad pitches; hit with power; avoid overstriding or pulling away from pitches as much as the hitter with a slower bat; and have good wrist action, which is the essence of power hitting.

The Minnesota Twins stress that a hitter's front shoulder must not open up too soon. They even take movies from center-field to show their hitters exactly when they are opening that front shoulder.

George Sisler, one of the all-time greats, felt that each hitter was an individual case, and that even perfect form was no guarantee of success. He felt that some hitters were too form-conscious and forgot why they were up at the plate—to hit the ball. That was the primary thing to remember; everything else had to be erased.

The batter had to be confident and re-laxed, never tense, and ready for any pitch. Sisler disapproved of guess-hitting.

To Sisler, the two basic factors in hitting were balance and timing. Everything related to them. The perfect way to hit was to have your weight equally distributed on both feet and have the bat moving at top acceleration at the moment of impact.

"I've observed that in all good hitters," he said, "the back foot stays in place from the start of the swing to the end."

He believed that the low pitch should be hit up, the high pitch down, and anything through the middle be hit with as level a swing as possible. He wanted the batter's arms to be back and well away from his body at the start of the swing, and his head and the bat had to be kept steady; unnecessary head and arm movements hindered good hitting.

Rogers Hornsby said, "A hitter who sticks his buttocks out will never become a great hitter, forget him. A fast bat is the hallmark of a truly great hitter."

Paul Richards believes that the good hitter must be able to stand up at the plate on close pitches. If he can't stand up there against pitchers who throw hard and are somewhat wild, he surely won't hit the ball. The fear of being hit is what brings the back foot up or off the ground.

A good eye implies the ability to lay off the pitch that you know you can't hit. Say the hitter has two balls and no strikes on him. He looks at the coach and gets the sign to hit. But even then he shouldn't swing unless he has the pitch timed perfectly.

Suppose it's a big change-of-pace that catches him off balance. If he goes ahead with his swing, he could pop up. The bad hitter will swing away and probably make an out.

This goes even up to two strikes. Why swing unless you have the pitch timed? If you don't have it timed, take it, as you certainly won't be able to do much with it.

When you get right down to it, the pitcher is in a rather tough spot when he is 2 and 0, 3 and 1, or 3 and 0. He not only has to get the ball over, but the umpire has to call it a strike, and that call isn't automatic.

So the hitter should let the pitcher pitch. The percentage is with him, if he'll make the most of it. If he doesn't, then the pitcher, with all the other percentages in his favor, certainly is going to have it over the hitter.

BATTING SLUMP

Here is some good advice from successful big-league players on how to break a batting slump:

Ted Williams advises that to break a slump, stand away from the plate and deep in the batter's box during batting practice so you can step across the box and hit the ball to the opposite field. This will force you to keep your head in there and watch the pitch.

Ty Cobb offered the following advice to slumping hitters: "Whenever you go into a slump, you're taking your eye off the ball, probably pulling your head away from it. You've got to watch the ball from the moment the pitcher rears back until the ball hits your bat or thumps into the catcher's mitt.

"The good hitter is always trying to hit every ball right back at the pitcher. So when you're in a slump just forget everything else and concentrate on driving that ball right back down the pitcher's throat. That will bring you out of the slump quicker than anything else."

Some big leaguers feel that by taking a great deal of extra batting practice, sometimes from a pitching machine, they will get their swing grooved again.

MAJOR LEAGUE HITTING LESSON

Harry Walker, one of the greatest hitting coaches of our time, took these fantastic hitting sequences of Willie McCovey, which show him hitting a home run on both the low pitch and high ball. This is really a master craftsman's study of the art of hitting. These are the finest pictures of hitting available for you to study and learn about hitting. Notice in these side-by-side pictures that everything is the same in the first five pictures of both the low pitch and the high pitch. You can't tell which is which. McCovey has executed all the sound mechanics perfectly and is waiting to see where the pitch is going and at what speed.

In the following paragraphs Harry Walker, the master hitting coach, will analyze these pictures for you; then study and restudy them until you understand all the mechanics of hitting and can put them into practice.

"Notice first McCovey is comfortable, and his hands are not too far away from his body, and they are back. Everything in baseball is balance and body control, including fielding, throwing, running, and hitting. In hitting, if you ever get your weight too far back, you are dead. You can't adjust. Hitting in plain words is nothing in the world but getting in a good set position where you can control the bat.

"The stride starts with the pitcher's arm. (Notice McCovey's stride is exactly the same on both pitches.) Time the arm, but keep your hands and hips back—like a set of triggers. If you commit yourself too quickly, you will be in trouble because you won't be able to adjust to the ball. (See how Willie is waiting and waiting.) A good hitter strides to get into position, waits, and adjusts to what the ball does. McCovey waits until he sees where the

pitch is going and whether it will be high or low; and then, notice the only adjustment is in the back leg, the real key to hitting. Notice on the high pitch how he barely bends his back leg, allowing his shoulders to stay level and to swing down on the ball. To illustrate this, stand up and spread your legs as far apart as possible. Now take an imaginary swing, and let your back leg buckle. Notice how the front shoulder goes up and the back elbow drops. This is one of the reasons for popping up all the time and for having trouble with the high pitch.

"In the low-pitch sequence note how Willie bends his back leg so he can go down and get it. Study this back leg adjustment because it's an important key to being an outstanding hitter. McCovey waits until he can see the pitch and what it's going to do. If he hadn't done this and had committed himself too soon, he couldn't adjust if the pitch turned out to be a sinker or change-up. You must be able to shift your weight properly from the back foot to the front one while not letting your back leg collapse. Take the same stride and follow through. To make sure you have a proper stroke on both pitches, hit fungoes to the outfield; hit fly balls and ground balls; and notice how your weight shifts and back leg adjusts. So, naturally, that back leg will allow you to stay on top of the ball with your swing.

"Bend your knees slightly to relax, and put the balls of your feet into a position where they can control the body. If you get back on your heels, you have no control. Your knees and back are like an elevator: They can go up and down. They help you get the bat to the ball and allow you to maneuver your hands and arms to where you can throw the barrel of the bat at the ball.

"Your hands and hips are still back. (Check McCovey pictures.) Once the hips come around, then your hands have to do all the work. Remember to bring that belly button around with the hands.

"Another drawback to locking the back leg is that you will be able to swing only with your hands instead of with your body. Keep the back leg comfortable, but do not let it buckle either. If the back leg buckles, the shoulder and the front elbow come up. This makes it tough to hit the baseball.

"As soon as you can, get the bat on the same plane with the ball. If you make an uppercut, there is only one spot where you can really make contact. On the other hand, you have nearly the entire length of the bat if you get the bat on the identical plane with the ball.

"Step up and into the ball when you hit. Now, you don't want to hit off the front foot although that's what a lot of people might think you are doing. Just hit off the back foot into the front foot.

"That front leg is stiff or slightly bent when that back leg comes through. Rather than hit and fall back, hit and follow through. When you throw a baseball, the weight begins on the back foot. As you stride forward, you throw into the front foot and push against that stiff front leg. Hitting follows the same theory. That front leg is slightly bent, and you hit into it.

"If your shoulder drops under the ball, then the high pitch will give you trouble. Remember to pick up the low ball and hit down on the high one. Pretend that you are 'chopping that top limb,' and let that back hip roll over.

"Remember to wait. Wait and then try to hit the ball through the middle of the diamond. Don't commit too soon."

You now have had a lesson from one of the real masters of hitting and one of the greatest hitting coaches in the history of the game. Study his ideas and come back to these pictures many times. The whole science and art of hitting is on these pages. Study and then go hit a baseball as often as you can.

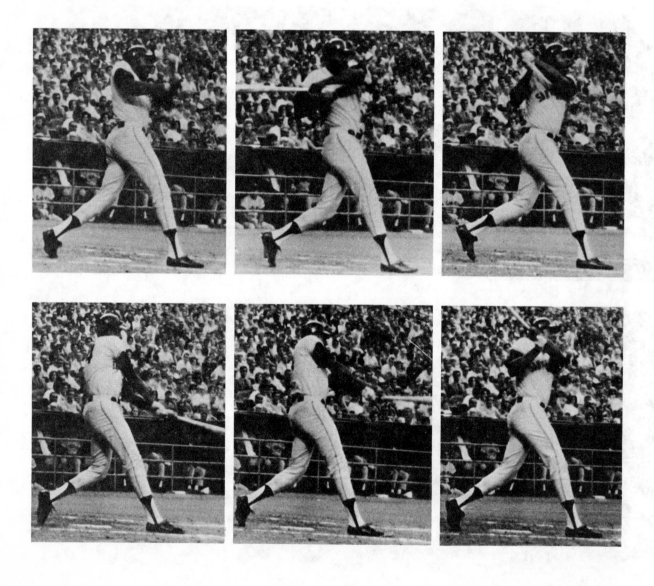

Jay Johnstone says, "Practice and practice some more in hitting from a batting tee. I just practice hitting the ball off the tee until I develop a stroke that becomes almost second nature. Using a batting tee is not just for Little Leaguers. It has real benefits at the highest level, too."

Make three of these tees for your own use; one at knee level, one waist high, and one shoulder high so that you can practice all three types of pitches. (For use in your own backyard the baseball can be replaced with a whiffle ball.)

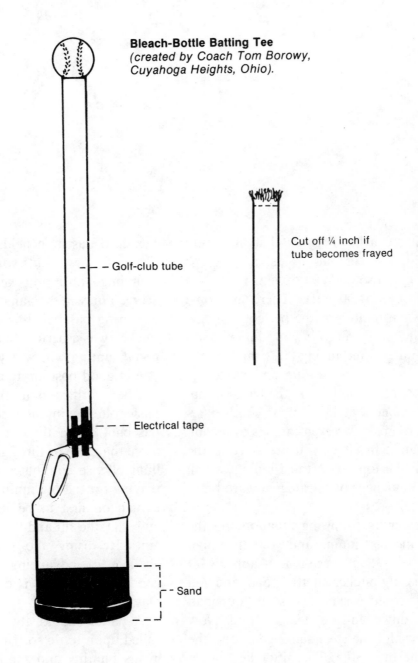

Bleach-Bottle Batting Tee
(created by Coach Tom Borowy, Cuyahoga Heights, Ohio).

— — Golf-club tube

Cut off ¼ inch if tube becomes frayed

— — — Electrical tape

Sand

chapter 8
BUNTING

Bunting can be the trick that makes an outstanding team out of just an average one. It can also add sixty points to a good bunter's batting average. There are some times when bunting is the perfect strategy. If a pitcher is retiring your hitters with ease, inning after inning, this might be a good time to start bunting and make the other team field and throw the ball around.

Remember that in a lot of youth baseball there are only seven innings to a complete game; in effect you are starting the game in the top of the third inning, which should influence your strategy toward bunting earlier.

Consider the following situation: It's the top of the last inning and your first man walks. Your team hasn't been able to hit the opposing pitcher all afternoon, and you haven't scored a run. You send your man on first down and he steals second. Now you give him the steal sign again, and the hitter the bunt sign. The hitter lays down a perfect bunt down the third base line,

the third baseman fields it and makes his throw to first; but your base runner is rounding third and keeps coming in to score. You win the game.

Daring baseball this sort of play is, but the key was a perfect bunt. Time and again good bunting will win you games or keep you in good position to challenge.

The sacrifice bunt must be a part of basic offense in high school and college baseball. Since these teams seldom have more than two or three good hitters, a good bunt offense eliminates the need for: (1) playing for the big inning, (2) considering a man on first to be in scoring position, and (3) the hit-and-run play, to some extent. By using the sacrifice bunt your chances of advancing runners are very good. A good bunt is difficult to field and play defensively.

A batter should always bunt when he's called upon to do so. He should take pride in his bunting and sacrifice himself when the occasion demands. A good bunter will have a deceptive bunting style and can boost his batting average with it, even though he may not be exceptionally fast.

THE SACRIFICE BUNT

Wait for the pitch with your knees bent. As the pitcher throws the ball, bring your back foot up about even with your front foot in a comfortable spread stance directly facing the pitcher. Hold the bat loosely in both hands and absolutely level, with top hand at the label and thumb and index finger forming a "V."

As the ball approaches, extend the bat in front of your body, then angle and draw it back toward your body, depending on whether you want to bunt down the first or third base line. (With a man on first, try to bunt down the first base line. With men on first and second, try to bunt hard enough down the third base line so that the third baseman, not the pitcher, will have to field the bunt.)

Let the ball hit the bat; don't push the bat at the ball. Make certain the pitch you bunt is a strike. An intelligent pitcher will try to make you pop up a high pitch if you try to bunt.

Don't break away from the plate too quickly; first be certain that the ball *has been bunted*.

BUNTING FOR A BASE HIT

A change-of-pace is the ideal pitch to bunt if it comes in low. A low fast ball can also be bunted for a base hit.

As the ball leaves the pitcher's hand, drop your rear foot back on a line at right

Bunting for a base hit, Willie Randolph style.

angles to the path of the ball (right-handed hitter). At the same time, slide your right hand up the bat slightly. Lower the bat to around hip level, angling it so as to drop the ball down the third base line (opposite for a left-handed hitter). Movement of the feet and lowering of the bat all come in one motion.

It is important on this bunt not to turn and face the pitcher. The hitter should keep the same relative body position as in the original stance.

Don't leave the batter's box until the ball is bunted on the ground. Well-placed bunts are easier to beat out than poorly placed bunts resulting from a fast getaway.

Another type of bunt a right-hander can use is a push bunt, in which, from normal batting stance, the ball is pushed just beyond the reach of the pitcher and toward the second baseman. This is also a good bunt to use for a sacrifice against a team whose pitcher and first baseman charge in rapidly to cover the bunt, and whose second baseman leaves his position entirely unguarded to cover first base. This is a particularly good maneuver in high school baseball.

The left-handed batter bunts much like the right-hander; but in order for the lefty to get the ball down the first base line, or past the pitcher and toward second, he must drag the ball around with his bat. This is called a drag bunt. (A drag bunt by a right-handed hitter would go toward third.) The lefty steps toward the pitcher as the ball leaves the pitcher's hand. The batter's hands need be moved only slightly up the bat, and the ball is literally dragged past the pitcher toward the second baseman.

To bunt down the third base line, the left-hander leans forward with bent knees, hardly moving his feet from his original stance, and angles his bat so as to drop

the ball down toward the third baseman. Again, it is important not to run away from the pitch in trying to get a fast start.

Bunting. Notice how the bunter has lowered his body, keeping his bat parallel with the ground.

THE SUICIDE SQUEEZE PLAY

This play is executed when there is a runner on third. The runner breaks for the plate as soon as the pitcher's arm reaches the release point. The hitter must bunt the ball, no matter where it is pitched, preferably toward the first baseman. He must learn to jump-shift just after the pitcher releases the ball. (Jump-shifting means bringing your feet parallel with a quick, short hop so that you are facing the pitcher and in correct bunting position.)

This is an excellent play for high school and young ball players. Practice it every day with every hitter. The pitcher who throws in the practice session should work from both the stretch and the wind-up position.

THE DOUBLE SQUEEZE PLAY

This play is executed when there are runners on second and third. Both runners break with the pitcher's motion to the plate. The batter bunts the pitch down the third base line. The runner on second should be rounding third by the time the bunt is being fielded. If the fielder makes a play for first, the runner continues home from third. With the runner on second in motion, this play allows the possibility of two runs scoring on a bunt.

THE FAKE BUNT

This is an excellent play for stealing. The idea is to try to draw an infielder out of position, or to give a base runner an extra split second to steal a base.

The bunter moves back in the batter's box to keep the catcher back with a fake. If the catcher moves forward, the hitter puts his bat out. This keeps the catcher back.

Cold, muddy days when it is impossible to hold regular practice are a good time to go outside and hold bunting practice. The pitcher, in bunting practice, should be a coach to avoid the risk of developing sore arms in pitchers.

BUNTING TIPS

Keep the bat level with the ground. Some coaches maintain that the bat should be held at a forty-five-degree angle, figuring that it is easier to keep the ball on the ground this way, avoiding pop-ups. But it is generally accepted that the level bat is best for young players.

Bunt only strikes.

Grip the bat lightly, and with hands apart. The top hand should slide along the barrel to the trademark; the bottom hand slides to the player's comfort or remains stationary.

Dip your knees slightly at impact to help deaden the roll of the ball. (In dipping the knees, the body acts like a spring, helping to take in the recoil from the impact.)

Bend down, with bent knees, for a low ball.

Bunt down the first base line to advance a runner to third. Rarely is a runner forced at third when the pitcher fields the ball on the first base side.

chapter 9
BASE RUNNING AND SLIDING

Touch or tag every base; never miss a bag.

Practice quick starting.

Get away fast at the plate and don't watch the ball. Keep your head down, in good running form.

Stay on base while looking for signs.

Get the habit of starting with a walking or running step to the next base as the ball is pitched. Don't be caught moving back to your base as the ball is pitched. This mistake is often made at third base.

Know how long a lead you can take and still return to the bag safely.

Watch the pitcher and take your lead as he steps on the rubber and starts up with his arms.

Take your lead with a sliding step, as is done in good defensive footwork in basketball.

Take your lead in almost a direct line to the next base. Don't drop behind the base line. The shortest distance between bases is a straight line.

A rule of thumb to follow in taking a lead at first is to be two steps and a slide away from the bag.

The only time to slide going into first is when the first baseman has been pulled off the bag by a bad throw and he attempts to tag you. Then, if a slide will avoid the tag, use it.

In rounding any base, pivot so you don't waste steps and cover more ground than necessary. You should be moving in an almost straight line toward the next base as you round any base. Pivot to the right by using a crossover step with the left leg about four strides in front of the base. Then bring the right leg back on a line toward the base you are approaching. Pivot in your natural stride; don't shorten up the last two or three steps trying to make the pivot. This takes practice.

It is best to tag the bag with your left foot on the inside corner as you round it, but don't break stride to do it. Hit the bag with your right foot if necessary to maintain stride.

BASE-RUNNING STRATEGY AND PSYCHOLOGY

Be alert and aggressive on the bases, ready to take advantage of any bobble or mistake by the opposition. But don't take foolish chances when you are behind. Always play the percentages.

Study the pitcher and catcher. Know what their habits and capabilities are. For example, a pitcher may have a high leg kick in his delivery; because his delivery will take a little longer, then, you may get a few extra steps before he releases the ball, making it much easier to steal a base.

Never loaf while running to a base. Run hard no matter how the ball is hit. There is always a chance for an error. *Nothing can be taken for granted in baseball.* Nothing looks more stupid to players and fans than to see a batter loaf to first on a pop-up or weak ground ball, and then make a sudden dash to the base when the ball is dropped or bobbled.

On a base hit to the outfield, make an aggressive turn at first and force the defense to hurry the throw—but *don't loaf coming back to the bag.*

Generally, advance a base when the lead runner advances.

The runner on third always tags up with his left foot when a fly ball is hit to the outfield with less than two down. The coach should not have to tell the runner when to leave after the catch; the runner can see this for himself, with the possible exception of a fly ball hit near the left field foul line. Then the runner should watch the coach for the sign to run.

Take your lead from third in foul territory to avoid being hit by a fair batted ball.

There is no excuse for a runner to be doubled off third on a *line drive to the infield or outfield.* In the first place, with less than two out the runner should not lead off any farther than the third baseman plays from the bag. In the second place, on any ball hit into the air, the runner should tag up immediately. If the ball is caught the runner will not be doubled then. If the ball

gets through the infield or bounces in the outfield, the runner can always score from third anyway.

On fly balls, runners on first and second should go halfway to the next base. In case the ball is dropped, lost in the sun or misjudged, he will be able to take full advantage of it. If the ball is hit very deep, the runners should tag up and advance after the catch.

It is not advisable for a runner to attempt to steal second base when a pitcher or a weak hitter is at bat. Failure to make the steal and being tagged out may cause the pitcher or weak hitter to become the first batsman for your team in the following inning. This is not good baseball.

On a double steal (with two outs and with men on first and third) the first base runner steals second, watching the defensive players at the base. If the ball coming from the catcher passes the player who is in the cut-off position and is caught by the player at second base, the runner never deliberately gives himself up for an easy put-out, but stops and runs back a few steps toward first. The reason for this is to allow the runner on third time to score before the put-out is made.

The runner on third should break for the plate as soon as he knows the catcher's throw is on its way to second, *if he has a good lead.* Or, if he did not break with the catcher's throw, he should break when the defensive player running the man down at second gets in a poor throwing position.

Don't get caught off third by the catcher on a bluff throw to second.

If you try to score from third on a ground ball and are obviously going to be thrown out at home, or are trapped between second and third with other runners on base, hold up and stall being tagged as long as possible to advance to scoring positions.

Always try to advance as far as possible when a teammate is trapped between bases —but don't get caught between bases yourself.

An important rule: A base runner should make every effort to reach third base when there is one man out, but he should never take the same chance to reach that base when no man is out or when two men are out.

Advice from coach Paul Richards: On a base line, a good base runner never needs help from a coach (but there are not very many really good base runners). In determining whether to score from second on a base hit, or to advance on a passed ball, make up your own mind. By the time the coach is able to decide, the opportunity may be gone. Going from first to third is a play for which a lot of base runners want help; in all the years I played baseball, I never looked to the coach for help on that particular play. I decided on the way from first to second how the ball was hit, where it was hit and who was throwing it, and that dictated to me whether I was going to try to get to third or not. Of course, the number of outs also had something to do with it. You never want to take a chance, if it is just a chance, with two out; with one out, yes; with no outs, that's great if you can make it.

BASE-RUNNING SITUATIONS

1. Runner on second, ball hit to third: The runner on second should have a safe lead—three steps and the length of the body, or three steps and a slide. He goes to third as the third baseman throws to first for the attempted out on the hitter.

2. Runner on first, base hit to the outfield: Just before the runner reaches second base, he looks at the ball as it is fielded. If the fielder is caught in a nonthrowing posi-

Baserunner is coming in with a pop-up slide.

Head-first slide, the quickest slide but one that leaves you open to injury.

Short, fade-away slide that makes it tougher for an infielder to tag you.

tion, the runner attempts to advance an extra base. The batter, rounding first, follows the runner ahead of him unless he sees a defensive player in a cut-off position, able to throw him out.

3. Runners on first and third: The first thought of the runner on third should be to try to score on any ball hit to the infield, in order to stop a double play if one is possible. Many times a double play is questionable, and the score is so close that the team on defense simply cannot give up another run. Then they may make the play at the plate (especially if there are no outs). If the ball thrown by the infielder reaches the catcher before the runner crosses the plate, the runner stops and runs back and forth until the runner on first has reached third and the batter has reached second.

4. Runners on second and third: The runner on third should try to score on any ground ball hit to the infield. If he sees that the throw beats him to the plate, he gets caught in a rundown and tries to give the runner behind him time to advance.

With runners on second and third, one out, and a fly ball hit to the outfield, the runner on second must be careful in tagging up and trying to advance after the catch. The throw may go to third and the runner there could be retired before the other runner crosses home plate.

5. Runner on third base only: When no one is out and the ball is hit toward an infielder, the runner should be sure the ball goes through to the outfield before attempting to score. If there is one out, the runner should try to score, and if the throw beats him, get caught in the rundown so the batter may advance to scoring position.

SLIDING

Bend the bottom leg, on which your weight rests, and slide only on the calf of

This is the way we like to steal home with a right-handed batter up.

that leg. Bend both legs, if you like, in learning. You probably have only one good side; just sit down and nature will put the right leg under for you. Most broken legs are caused by sliding on bad sides.

Tag with the top leg, which should be held loose and relaxed.

Hook with the top leg when sliding. Shove top leg straight when going in on a straight-in slide. This is the quickest way to get to base.

To learn sliding, start with short distances to be sure that your leg can be bent. Then gradually you can lengthen your distance. Speed will follow—a must for all good slides.

Keep low to the ground, neither leaping or jumping. Sliding is like gliding.

Throw your head back as you bend both legs. This will prevent your knees from hitting the ground first.

Start your slide at least six to eight feet from the bag. Do not slide late. Keep the bag loose for this reason until you learn to space yourself. If you keep sliding late, just raise your body as you hit the bag. This will take the jar away. This is only temporary; a slider should learn to do it right.

Always slide going into second, third, or

home if there is any possible play on you. Never take for granted the throw might go elsewhere. Sliding saves valuable seconds and keeps you from overrunning the base and being tagged off it.

To do a pop-up slide (pop up on your feet again to continue running to the next base), raise your body up from the waist as you slide along with speed; a slight push of your hands will bring your body up. It is the speed that does it.

Practice every day.

SLIDING TIPS

Remove shoes to prevent injury while you're practicing. Run in your stocking feet or tennis shoes.

Use a dry lawn or short lawn as a sliding pit.

Use practice pants over clean uniform to prevent soiling and annoying strawberry (skin burning on side from sliding too much on side and not on calf of bent leg).

Always use sliding pads, made of light, slick material such as nylon.

Hold grass in each hand so you will not reach back to brace yourself with your hands as you hit the ground, and injure yourself.

Use a rope to teach yourself to keep your body low—stretch a rope about four feet above the ground and have two boys hold it as players slide under it to keep low. Holders release the rope if player slides too high.

chapter 10
RUNDOWNS

There's nothing like a well-executed pick-off or cutoff play to give a team a lift. It's the kind of play that can kill a potentially big inning or rally and save or turn around a ball game.

Conversely, there's nothing more discouraging than to catch a runner and then botch the play, permitting the trapped man to get back safely or, worse, advance a base through a dropped throw, being hit by the ball, or a fielder's obstruction. One major league manager once spent a great deal of spring training time teaching runners in rundown or hot-box situations to deliberately run into an infielder as soon as he made a throw.

We begin our rundown practice early in the year and continue working on it throughout the season. We have our entire squad work on the play so everybody will know how to handle it both offensively and defensively.

In executing the play, we observe the following rules:

1. Try to get the runner with as few throws as possible.

2. When you get the ball, grip it barehanded in an overhand position, ready to throw.

3. In preparing to receive a throw, stand in the infield side of the base line to reduce the possibility of the throw hitting the runner.

4. Immediately after throwing, veer out of the base line in order to prevent obstruction. Then back up the man you threw to.

5. Don't use voice signals. When you want the ball and can make the tag, take two steps toward the runner. This should be the signal for your teammate to throw to you.

6. In making the tag—with either hand—give with the runner in the direction in which he's moving. This helps eliminate the possibility of his knocking the ball out of your hand.

7. When there's more than one base runner, go after one and make the tag as

77

Notice in the first photo how the infielder gets the runner going full speed back to the base he came from. Then in photo 2 he holds his hand up high enough so his teammate can see it and gives him a soft toss. In the last picture notice how the infielder makes the tag and gets his glove up to keep the ball from getting knocked loose.

quickly as possible to prevent the other runner(s) from advancing.

8. If you feel that an overhand throw will hit the runner, step to the side and throw sidearm.

9. Remember, you cannot block the base path without the ball (this is obstruc-

tion), and that if two runners are on the same base, it belongs to the lead runner.

10. If you're the front man in the rundown and have the ball, run hard at the runner to force him back toward his original base.

11. After a successful pick-off at first,

the shortstop, who's moving toward the runner in a direct line with the first baseman, should be the lead man. The second baseman should cover second, backing up the shortstop.

Whenever possible, we want our players to stand about three or four feet in front of the bag. This is an advantage on a late throw. If the tag must be made at the base, our man will still have a chance to make the play. If he were farther away, the late throw would cost him the putout. It's vital to stay out of the runner's way when someone else has the ball.

We don't go for excessive arm-and-ball faking. It can fool the other infielders just as readily as the runner. If you must fake, we suggest using only one motion, to let the receiver know that he'll get the ball on the next motion. The throw should, incidentally, be soft.

The following plays are excellent for setting up rundown situations:

1. Runners on first and third—pitcher bluffs a pick-off move to third, wheels, and fires to first to trap the runner.

2. In an obvious bunt situation (runners on first and second) or with the runner on first representing an important run, call for a curve ball on the first-base side of the plate. The first baseman charges hard and the second baseman sneaks in behind the runner at first for a pick-off throw from the catcher.

3. With the pick-off in order at second, the catcher comes out in front of the plate and raises his hand or talks it up. This initiates the play. When the catcher squats for his signs, he touches his left shin guard with his bare hand to inform the shortstop to cover. The pitcher checks the runner and looks in to the catcher. When the catcher feels the runner is vulnerable, he throws both hands open quickly and the pitcher turns and fires to second.

chapter 11
JEFF TORBORG ON CATCHING

Catching is the hub of the defense. One of the finest catchers in recent history is Jeff Torborg, who handled one of the best pitching staffs of all time, Koufax, Drysdale, Sutton, Osteen, and Regan. Besides being a fine receiver he has the ability to really teach catching.

Jeff, what is a good sign giving stance?

Take your right knee and point it right at the pitcher. Also, have the left knee pointing at your pitcher with the glove shading over the knee. Koufax gave up back-to-back homeruns in Pittsburgh once due to a sign-giving stance mistake. I didn't have a sweatshirt on, revealing my arm-muscle movements every time I gave the sign. After that, I had to wear a long-sleeve sweatshirt to cover my arm.

How would you teach and work with a young boy who wants to be an outstanding catcher?

1. First there is a squatting drill where you

work near a fence to grab onto for balance.
2. Work on the young man getting his rump up; in this way he can move to get the high pitch. Don't get too low as this will also tie up your head and neck.
3. Bare hand back of glove at least first two fingers.
4. While giving a target, don't lock your wrist, be in the ready position and give a soft target.
5. Ready stance:
   a. Mitt down like a shovel.
   b. Receive the ball; don't jab at it.
6. If a catcher caught the ball and never dropped a pitch, congratulate him.

How would you teach throwing from behind the plate? Major league catchers have told me you have a beautiful way of teaching it.

In teaching throwing, we want the weight on the right foot. I like to compare it to archery. The catcher's throw is like

Carlton Fisk gives a great lesson for catchers in this sequence. Notice how close he sets up behind the hitter and how in the first picture he hides the sign perfectly. In the second picture he shows with his bare hand the location for the next pitch (low and outside). Note the perfect low target even though Fisk is a big man. Notice as he receives the ball his arms are outside his legs to allow free movement. Are there men on base? Why do you feel there are or are not?

shooting an arrow. Pull your right elbow straight back to the right shoulder. Then sight down the bow, keeping your left arm straight and pointing the glove in the direction where you want to throw.

1. If you move your glove, your body will come over.
2. Elbow up and back like pulling a bow.
3. Do not bring ball to ear to throw.

Jeff demonstrated a good drill to teach a catcher to grip the ball across the seams. With a catcher's mitt and a ball, he just sits down, reaches into his glove four fingers across, catches the ball. Then he changes to two fingers across seams, reaches back, breaks his hands, and points his elbow to his shoulder, all this time trying to keep his bare hand relaxed.

Another point in working with catchers is to be sure their shoulders are straight in the direction they're trying to throw. If you open your shoulders you lose body power and velocity on the throw.

Jeff, your way of teaching the jump step is a classic for catchers. How do you teach it?

Catch the ball and jump; right foot will jump to the left. Tell each catcher to act as though he has a barber pole running through the middle of his body so that he'll jump up and pivot to get the shoulders straight and get a quicker release on his throw. Try to throw with the least number of steps. Your throwing position is like a punching position. In the jump shift, try to click the right heel together with your left heel.

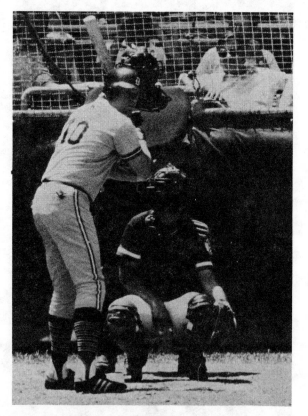

In these pictures from center field, notice how the catcher has taped his fingers to make it easier for the pitcher to see the signs. This is a great idea, especially in night games when you have a pitcher on the mound with eye problems.

chapter 12
PLAYING INFIELD

Infielders should shift their normal positions, depending on what hitter is at the plate. Generally, right-handed hitters hit to left field and left-handed hitters hit to right field. There are exceptions to this; observation and scouting reports can help infielders learn how to play different hitters.

GENERAL TIPS

Keep your arms and hands off your knees in the starting position. Your feet should be apart with your weight equally balanced on both feet.

Watch the ball all the way from the pitcher's hand to the plate.

Never leave a base uncovered.

On all bobbles, look for runners overrunning bases.

Whenever possible, the second baseman, shortstop, and third baseman should straddle the bag and tag the runner out; never go out to meet a runner. Tag the bag with your ball and glove, letting the runner tag

himself out. Always use the back of your wrist to avoid being kicked and losing the ball.

Baseball is a team game, and you should know the strengths and weaknesses of your infield mates: the ground they can cover, the strength of their arms, and their speed. Be willing to make up for any qualities lacking in your fellow players by covering extra ground, calling for plays, backing up throws, and yelling helpful advice, such as, "Take your time!"

Learn to keep your hands well in front of you and close to the ground while fielding a ball. You can pull your hands up quicker than you can drop them. Do not fight the ball with rigid hands; be relaxed.

Throwing accurately is most essential. Be sure to step forward when you make a throw.

Always anticipate a coming play or situation. Make up your mind where you will throw the ball if it is hit to you.

The entire infield should play close in to

In this sequence a major league infielder shows perfect throwing form. Notice in the second picture how Doug Flynn gets that ball right up to his ear very quickly for a fast release (like pulling a bow back instead of winding up), along with a short crow hop and a splendid follow-through in the last pictures.

cut off the runner at the plate, if it is the tying or winning run late in the game. Never play close in during the early innings or in a lopsided game.

Do not throw the ball if there is no chance of getting your man. Bluff the peg; you may catch someone else trying to take an extra base on the expected throw.

On extra base hits to the outfield, the second baseman acts as relay man on balls hit to right and right center; the shortstop covers second base. The shortstop acts as relay man on balls hit to left and left center; the second baseman covers second. On balls hit directly to center field, the infielder with the best arm acts as the relay man. The first baseman acts as relay man on all extra base hits along the right field foul line whenever there is a chance of a man scoring.

Make short, accurate throws.

Keep your wrists loose and bring every ball in to your body. Stiff wrists cause fielders to stab at balls.

Charge the ball, but slow up the last twenty feet and widen your base so you can change direction if the ball goes to one side or the other. Keep your feet wide apart on this play.

Play the arc on hard-hit ground balls.

Use a short-fingered flat glove to keep the ball from sticking in the webbing, and use the glove hand to slap the ball into the bare or throwing hand to get rid of it quickly.

Watch to see that base runners touch each base.

TIP FOR THE COACH

A good drill for infielders is to have them field ground balls with just their glove hand, keeping their bare hand behind them.

Brett is in a perfect position to break in any direction as the ball is hit. In photo 2 Brett has the weight on the balls of his feet, arms away from his body, knees flexed, and hands relaxed in front of him. Then he really reacts instantly as the ball is hit.

chapter 13
PLAYING FIRST BASE

NORMAL POSITION OF PLAY

Take your position in the infield so you can reach the bag and receive a throw with no extra effort. If a hitter is exceptionally slow, play deeper than usual. If a hitter is fast, play in closer; anticipate a bunt.

Face all infielders for all throws. Keep your knees slightly bent and be ready for a high throw. Take high throws with a short jump and an open glove. When the ball hits your glove, close it immediately.

To catch balls on the bounce, have your hands moving toward you. Multiple-bounce balls take a great deal of practice. Be sure to hold your glove open and still; don't swipe at the ball.

As soon as the ball is hit to any other infielder, break immediately for the bag. Take your position in front of the bag with your feet stationary, astride the bag. Be able to shift instantly in either direction if the ball is thrown wide.

On balls thrown wide to the left of the bag, shift your position so that your right foot is in contact with the bag and your left

This is the major league way to stretch and cut down on the time for a double play or a close play at first.

A first baseman should be of medium height, with a good reach. He must be able to maintain perfect balance on his feet and to shift easily. He must have extraordinary ability in making low-thrown pickups. He should be able to throw sidearm for the force-out at second base. He can be either right- or left-handed, though a left-handed first baseman has the advantage on tag plays and the throw to second base.

86

foot is extended as far as possible from the bag. On balls thrown wide to the right of the bag, shift your feet so that your left foot is in contact with the bag and your right foot extended as far as possible from the bag. Always remember that the most important thing is to catch the ball.

Stretch as far as possible to meet the ball for anticipated close plays.

The hardest play for a first baseman is a ball thrown on the left of the bag, directly in the path of the base runner. If there is time to step completely off the bag and catch the ball and then tag the runner, do so.

If the throw is right to the bag, and if you are left-handed, keep your left foot on the bag and extend your right foot; if you are right-handed keep your right foot on the bag and extend your left foot.

When you tag a base runner, close your hand tightly over the ball. Let your hand

Willie Stargell demonstrates perfect fielding form for a first baseman—crouched, alert as a cat, and weight forward.

move in the direction the base runner is moving, so you don't injure your hand making a hard tag-out.

If there is plenty of time on a high ball, take a step back into foul territory, keeping your right foot on the bag if you are right-handed, or your left foot on the bag if you are left-handed. Reach high into the air for the catch.

Try for every ball you can possibly reach. The second baseman will chase you away if you attempt to field a ball too close to him. When the second baseman shouts, "I've got it!" return immediately to your bag.

When you go for a ball, the pitcher covers first. When you throw to him as you lead him toward first base, throw under-handed, shoulder-high, as you stride toward the bag. When you field the ball deeply, and the pitcher comes to a complete stop at first base, ready to catch like a first baseman, throw overhanded.

Bluff a cut-off; it will often make a base runner going to second hesitate.

POSITION OF PLAY IN OTHER SITUATIONS

Man on first base

Stand with your right foot on the inside edge of the bag. When the pitcher throws to catch the runner, catch the ball and touch the runner with a sweeping motion. The instant the ball is pitched, take two or three steps toward second base and float by jumping through the air and coming down in a set position on both feet. (The purpose is to be perfectly balanced on both feet and ready to move in any direction to field the batted ball.)

Runner on first base and the situation prompts a bunt

Move from the bag toward the plate, but not too quickly. If the batter bunts down

Willie Stargell illustrates perfectly how to charge home plate in a bunt situation. This is a key play for the first baseman to learn so that he can get the lead runner or poorly executed bunt and kill a rally.

the first base side of the field, charge quickly toward the ball and try for a possible force play at second base. If there is no chance for a play at second, throw to the second baseman, who covers first base. On bunts toward third base, return to the bag to make the put-out. After the put-out, run into the infield to help break up any attempt by the runner to advance to third base. When the pitcher fields the bunted ball, return to the bag, if possible, to make the play; otherwise, the second baseman takes the throw from the pitcher.

Runner on second base

Play your normal position.

Runners on first and second bases

If a bunt is in order, play in close, halfway between the pitcher's box and first base. If the ball is bunted, field the ball and throw it to the base called by the catcher.

If a bunt is not in order, play in your normal position.

For a double play starting from first base, always field the ball facing the middle of the diamond. If you are left-handed, throw overhanded to second base. If you are right-handed, make a jump pivot turn on your right foot as you field the ball and make a quarter turn with your back to the center of the diamond. Throw overhanded to the second baseman. Then return quickly to first base to receive the throw, which completes the double play. Throw inside second base when you throw to the shortstop, if he's covering second base.

TIPS FOR COACHES

The best drill for teaching first basemen to catch multiple-bounce balls is to have them throw balls into the dirt to each other at various spots, in various directions. They should catch a hundred balls a day from about forty feet away.

An excellent drill to teach footwork is to have first basemen practice shifting and stretching at home with a cardboard base.

chapter 14
PLAYING SECOND BASE

A second baseman should be fast on his feet, possess quick reflexes, and have the ability to get rid of the ball quickly, to throw accurately from any position, and to make a double play. He should be able to throw sidearm, underhand and overhand.

Both hands are down. Arms and hands are ready to cradle the ball.

NORMAL POSITION OF PLAY

Play shallow or deep, according to the batter's speed and the condition of the playing field—wet and slow, or dry and fast.

POSITION OF PLAY IN OTHER SITUATIONS

Runner on first base, or runners on first and second, and the hitter is expected to bunt

Move in toward the plate and shade toward first base, ready to make the put-out at first in the event that the first baseman cannot get back to the bag in time to make the throw. If he does, you back up his throw.

Don't break toward first base before the ball is actually bunted. If you break too soon, the batter might push the ball to the spot you leave vacant.

With runners on first and second, nobody out, instead of having the second baseman covering first, some teams are having their first baseman cover first and their second baseman charge the first base line and field the bunt.

Runner on first base, one or no outs, a double play in sight, right-handed batter at the plate

Close in by taking two or three steps directly toward home plate and a shade toward second. (But when the batter is definitely a left-handed pull-hitter, you should figure that he will get the ball off the bat, so start the play yourself.)

Runners on first and third bases, attempted double steal in order, right-handed batter at the plate

When a double steal is attempted, run quickly from your position, after the ball has gone past the hitter, to approximately one step in front of second base, in a direct line with home plate. Watch for an attempt by the runner on third base to score. If he breaks for the plate, charge fast to cut off the catcher's throw and return the ball

to the catcher. If the runner on third does not attempt to score, wait in position, one step in front of second base, for the catcher's throw and then pivot around to make the tag at second base.

There is another method of play recommended for the same situation. The second baseman runs rapidly from position to a spot halfway between the pitcher's box and second base, directly in line with home plate. As he comes into this position, he watches for the third base runner to attempt to score. If he breaks for the plate, catch the ball thrown by the catcher and return it to the plate for a possible put-out. If the runner does not make a break for the plate, let the ball go through to the shortstop, who is covering second base, for the put-out on the runner coming from first base.

Remember that the score of the game

This is the way to make the tag at a second. The infielder in photo 1 has both hands together; his body is bent; and he is behind and stradling the bag. As he gets the ball, he puts the back of the glove down and lets the runner tag himself out. Then in the last photos he pulls his glove hand out so the ball won't get knocked loose.

and the inning will determine whether you should try to cut the runner off at the plate or try to get the runner stealing second base. If the run is the winning or tying run, the play should be made to the plate.

METHOD OF PLAYING SECOND BASE

Move in on all batted balls, except hard-hit balls; never wait for the ball to reach you. Try to play the hops; don't let the ball play you.

Field the ball with relaxed hands. Keep your glove and bare hand facing the ball, well in front of you and close to the ground. Keep your head down, eyes on the ball, feet apart, and weight balanced.

Most ground balls hit near first base, if they are fielded by the second baseman, should be thrown, underhand or sidearm, to the first baseman. On this type of play yell, "I've got it!" to let the first baseman know you can make the play. On ground balls hit directly to you at second base, field the ball, straighten up, take a short step, and throw overhand to first base.

On balls hit to your extreme right, go full speed for the ball. Throw your weight on your right foot and brace yourself as quickly as possible. Balance for the throw to first base, using your best overhanded throw for carry and accuracy.

On slow-hit rollers, charge the ball, scoop it up barehanded while you're still on the run, and throw the ball in an underhanded motion.

MAKING A DOUBLE PLAY

Get to the bag as quickly as possible. Have your bare hand by your gloved hand; this saves a split second. Touch the bag with either foot, then throw with something on the ball. Always take a short hop with both feet after throwing the ball; this gets the weight off your legs and prevents seri-

In this remarkable sequence the second baseman is making one of the toughest plays possible at second, a force play with a bad throw. Notice how the infielder is in a crouched position behind the bag. In the second picture he backhands and stretches way out, still keeping contact with the bag and getting the force out on a really difficult play.

ous injury in case the man coming from first runs into you.

A great deal depends on the position of the pivot man before the ball is hit, the speed of the runner coming into second base, the speed of the batted ball, and the type of throw the pivot man will receive from the infielder.

In all cases, the second baseman quickly makes his break for second base, timing himself so that the instant before he reaches the bag, his feet are spread and he is on balance. If the throw is to his right, he can, from this position, shift to his right and touch the bag with his left foot; if the throw is to his left, he can shift to his left and touch the bag with his right foot. He should throw the ball in his most comfortable manner, which is governed by the type of play and his ability to get rid of the ball.

An important point is to be sure both hands are together to receive the throw; it is much quicker to get rid of the ball this way. This is the reason some professional second basemen use a pancake glove and slap the ball into the bare hand to make the throw.

FIELDING FLY BALLS

Field all flies you can reach in back of first base. Try for every fly ball hit in any direction, but once another player calls for the catch, return immediately to second base.

The sun plays an important part in pop-ups, and the entire infield must get together as the game goes along to determine who should take the pop-ups in each area. You should know where the outfielders are playing at all times. Allow an outfielder to catch any pop-ups he can reach; it is much easier for an outfielder to catch a ball coming in than it is for an infielder to catch it going away.

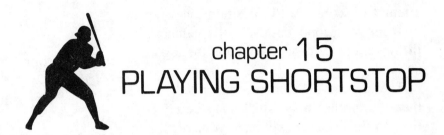

chapter 15
PLAYING SHORTSTOP

A shortstop should have a strong arm; if his arm is not too strong, he must develop the art of getting the ball away fast on all throws. This is accomplished by not using any wasted motion. He must be loose and limber, and any boy with a stiff back will be handicapped in this position.

NORMAL POSITION OF PLAY

Distribute your territory so that you can go to the right or left equally well.

POSITION OF PLAY IN OTHER SITUATIONS

Runner on first base, no one out, a close score, and a bunt is anticipated

Move in a step or two directly in line with home plate and a few steps closer to second base. Be ready to go to second base to make the force-out if the play is made to second. Try to make this play like a first baseman, stretching out as far as possible. (This is true on all force-out plays at second base.)

Runners on first and second bases, no one out, a cinch bunt in order

Move in directly in back of the base runner, a few feet off second base, but don't leave your fielding position too vulnerable. Your main duty is to keep the base runner close to second base to prevent him from getting too big a lead in case there is a bunt and a possible force play at third base.

Runner on first base, no one out, a double play in sight, and a left-handed batter at the plate

Move in a few steps directly toward home plate and a shade toward second base before the pitcher takes his position on the rubber; this keeps you from losing too much time getting to second base. It is all-important to get to the bag in time to start a double play.

Runners on first and third bases, a double steal attempt anticipated, and a left-handed batter at the plate

If a double steal is attempted, run rapidly from your position after the ball has gone by the hitter to approximately one step in front of second base, in a direct line with home plate. Watch for an attempt by the runner on third base to score. If the runner breaks for the plate, charge fast to cut off the catcher's throw and return the ball to him. If the runner on third does not attempt to score, wait in position, one step in front of second base, for the catcher's throw and pivot around to make the tag at second.

The method above is recommended, but there is another play which may be effective. In this, run quickly from your regular position to a spot about halfway between the pitcher's box and second base, directly in line with home plate. Watch for an attempt by the runner on third base to score. If the runner breaks for the plate, catch the ball thrown by the catcher and return it to the plate for a possible put-out. If the runner doesn't make a break for the plate, you'll be in position to let the ball go through to the second baseman, who is covering his base, to put out the runner coming from first base.

Again, always remember that the score and the inning of the game will determine if you should try to cut the runner off at the plate or try to get the runner stealing second base. If the run is the winning or tying run, the play should be made to the plate.

Runner on second base, one out, close score, a left-handed batter at the plate

Shorten up your position, faking the runner back to second base now and then. Your main function on this play is to keep the runner close to the bag, preventing an easy steal to third and cutting down the chances for scoring on a short single.

METHOD OF PLAY

Move in on all ground balls. Play the ball; don't let the ball play you. Be directly in front of the ball, your legs apart, ready to get into good throwing position. Straighten up, take a short step to regain balance and throw, stepping in the direction of your throw. Don't ever lob the ball; put something on it. Be sure your hands and glove are close to the ground when fielding ground balls. Keep your hands relaxed.

When you field the ball near second base to make a force play, take a step or two toward second as you toss the ball underhanded. Make sure your throws to the second baseman are above the waist.

Your most difficult fielding plays are made: (1) when a hit ball bounds over the pitcher's head and (2) when a ball is hit to the left of the third baseman and to your extreme right. In the first case, field the ball on the run. Throw to first base under full speed, in the position from which you field the ball. It is impossible to set yourself up for a perfect throw, but practice will help in this play.

In the second case, go after the ball at full speed. As you field it, throw most of your weight on your right foot to slide some distance in the dirt. Brace yourself for this. As quickly as possible, balance your body for the throw to first base. As you come up with the ball, quickly sneak a look at the first baseman to see if you can throw in time to make the out. (This also helps you pick up your target earlier.) Then make an overhanded throw.

On hard-hit balls that come directly to you, field the ball, straighten up and take a short step to regain balance. If time allows, take a step or two in the direction of the base, throwing overhanded with good stuff on the ball, for accuracy and carry. Do not hurry this throw if time allows. Hurried throws are usually wild.

FIELDING FLY BALLS

The sun plays a very important part in pop-ups, and the entire infield must get together, as the game goes along, to determine who should take the pop-ups when the ball is hit in each area. The shortstop should at all times know where the outfielders are playing and allow the outfielder to catch a ball coming in. It is much easier for an outfielder than for the infielder to get a ball moving out toward the outfield. You should take all fly balls, fair or foul, that the left fielder does not call for, in back of the third baseman. You take all throws from the pitcher on balls hit directly back to the pitcher when the play is to second base. The only exception to this is when the hitter is a definite right-handed pull-hitter, and the shortstop is playing to the extreme right of his normal position. The second baseman then takes the throw.

DOUBLE PLAYS

Double plays made with the second baseman fielding the ball and the shortstop acting as the pivot, and vice versa, are perfect examples of proper teamwork and coordination.

The main defense in making double plays is to be sure that the man who will make the pivot, depending on whether the batter is right- or left-handed, plays close enough in, or near second base, so he can reach second in time to receive the throw, tag the bag, and get rid of the ball before the base runner, coming from first, has a chance to break up the play. Be sure to line yourself up as soon as possible behind the bag to give the shortstop a line on the throw.

Executing the double play perfectly is illustrated in this sequence. The shortstop gets a perfect feed from the second baseman, shuffles across the bag, plants his lead foot, and makes a perfect throw. then he takes a little hop on both feet to get his weight to the top part of his body so that, if the runner bowls him over, he cuts down on the chance of injuring himself.

All throws in, around, or close to second base should be made underhanded. It is well for the shortstop or second baseman to receive this throw an instant before his foot hits the bag.

All longer throws, by either you or the second baseman, should be made by a forearm, a modified overhand, or a sidearm throw, to save time. All throws should be made above the waist. When you are to receive the throw from the second baseman on a double play, you should attempt to receive the ball an instant before your foot hits the bag. You step past the bag with your left foot, then you drag your right foot or toe across the bag, throw the ball in the same motion, and then hop. When the shortstop is to receive the throw from the first baseman on a double play, you should take the throw inside the bag, coming to a quick stop as you hit the bag with your left foot. Make a forearm throw back to first base, but give the first baseman time to retrace his steps. When the second baseman is to receive the throw from the shortstop or third baseman on a double play, he should get to the bag quickly; he then has a choice of many ways to tag the bag.

A great deal depends on the position of the pivot man before the ball is hit, the speed of the runner coming into second base, the speed of the batted ball, and the type of throw the pivot man will receive from the infielder.

chapter 16
PLAYING THIRD BASE

A third baseman must have quick hands and very fast reflexes. He must not be afraid of hard-hit ground balls. He must be willing to take tough hops that he misses with his glove. He must have a good arm and the ability to throw overhanded. When he fields a ball, he must be sure his hands are down on the ground, with no room for the ball to go through. He should be able to knock down balls, pick them up and still throw the runner out. A third baseman generally has more time to field and throw a batted ball than any other infielder; he should take advantage of this opportunity by not hurrying his throw.

NORMAL POSITION OF PLAY

Generally the third baseman plays three or four steps away from the bag and even with it. However, his position depends entirely on the ball and strike count on the hitter, and the score and inning of the game.

The third baseman is as ready as a cat, making a slight movement as the ball reaches the plate.

POSITION OF PLAY IN OTHER SITUATIONS

Defensive position against a right-handed pull-hitter

Play deep and protect the line by playing closer to it. Make sure that no fair ball can go between you and the line.

Runner on first base, no one out, a bunt in order or a known bunter at bat, or someone who is very fast

Play a step or two ahead of third base into the diamond. Move in as the pitcher delivers the ball.

Runner on first or second base, no one out, a bunt in order

This is a difficult play for the average third baseman to make. A great deal depends on the fielding ability of the pitcher, and the teamwork of the pitcher and the third baseman. Ordinarily, when the third baseman and the pitcher try to decide who will field the ball, confusion and wild throws are the only result.

Play a step or two into the diamond ahead of third base. Charge all bunts and make the put-out at first or second base, depending on the catcher's call. Remember another play might follow immediately. If the bunt is directly back to the pitcher, or if the pitcher is an exceptionally good fielder and calls for the play, retrace your steps and be prepared for the possible force-out at third base.

Runner on second base, bunt possible

Play ahead of third base into the diamond, and, if the hitter fails to bunt, come back to third base to protect it from a possible steal.

Try to field all balls that you can reach, even though some seem to be hit at the shortstop, particularly on slow-hit balls. On these, field on the run and throw overhand to first base, all in one motion.

Always watch the hitter, not the pitcher, while the ball is being pitched. You will find you can get a better jump on the ball by doing this, and it enables you to get a much better start on the ball if the batter tries to bunt.

On balls hit directly back to the pitcher, always make your break to the middle of

In this attempted tag at third base, is the runner safe or out? Where do you think the throw came from? Why?

the infield, in order to be in position to field deflected balls.

Take all fly balls between third base and the catcher.

Back up the pitcher on all return throws from first base on attempted pick-off plays.

Another good play for a third baseman with a runner on second and no chance to get the batter is to fake a throw to first, wheel and try to tag the base runner coming to third.

TIPS TO THE COACH

A good drill for teaching a third baseman to charge slow-hopping tapped balls is to line up a string of eight to ten balls in a straight line from home plate halfway to third base. Have him play his normal position and charge full speed, picking up the first ball with his bare hand and throwing to first. He returns to his starting position and repeats the exercise.

chapter 17
PLAYING OUTFIELD

An outfielder must be a good judge of a fly ball, have the ability to "get a jump" on a batted ball, be fast afoot and possess a good overhand throwing arm.

The center-fielder covers the greatest amount of territory. Therefore, he should be able to start quickly on fly balls, throw well for distance and field in all directions, front, back, left, and right.

The center-fielder has the best view of the distance between the batter and the plate, and he can follow the course of the pitched ball over the plate, which is beneficial for a quick start; therefore, very few center-fielders need the signal assistance when fast, curve, or slow balls are pitched.

The center-fielder should be the outfield quarterback. He should take complete charge and claim every hit ball, until it is taken off by the right- or left-fielder by a yell or arm motion.

The left- and right-fielders should shift with the center-fielder against all pull-hitters.

FLY BALLS

Get under the ball as quickly as possible.

Be *relaxed;* don't reach out until you're almost under the ball.

Balls above your waist should be caught with palms straight out or lifted toward the moving ball.

If the ball is over your head, turn according to the wind and run; don't run backward.

Never stop if you have a chance of catching the ball.

GROUND BALLS

Get in front of the ball.

If there is a play at a base, line up with the play and try to take it in stride.

THROWS

Always be set, and use a full arm throw.

Use a bounce about fifty feet from the plate on a throw to the catcher.

Ken Griffey gets the most out of his arm and body on this throw from the outfield. In the first photo, he throws from over the top with everything going into the throw. Look at the cords in his neck. Photo 2 shows how he put his whole body behind the throw.

Throw one base ahead of the runner, unless you're close to the base he's approaching.

IMPORTANT DEFENSIVE PLAYS

Right-fielder backs up first base on all bunted balls.

Right-fielder backs up second base on all balls thrown from the left side of the diamond.

The center-fielder backs up second base on all bunts and on all attempted outs at the bag.

The left-fielder backs up second base on all attempted outs from the right side of the diamond, and he backs up third on all attempted outs at that bag.

With a straightaway hitter, the outfielders should divide the space between the foul lines equally among them.

With a left-field hitter, the left-fielder plays closer to the line, the center-fielder moves into left center, and the right-fielder goes to right center, but not too deep.

With a right-field hitter, the right-fielder plays close to the line, the center-fielder plays right center, and the left-fielder plays left center field, but not too deep.

If a hard wind is blowing toward the infield, fielders play in. If a hard wind is blowing out, play deeper. A crosswind causes the ball to curve.

SUGGESTIONS

An outfielder must know where a runner is so that he can throw the ball immediately after catching it.

Throw on a line.

When two outfielders are in a position to catch a fly, the one who is in the best position to throw after the catch should make the catch.

An outfielder throws the first relay about shoulder-high.

Get rid of the ball quickly. Keep both hands together when you catch the ball.

If you are weak on running back to get deep fly balls, you should play deeper.

When you catch a fly ball close to the infield with runners on, immediately run toward infield.

Fly balls that can be taken by both infielders and outfielders should be taken by an outfielder; and he should shout, "I have it," to let the others know how to play the defense.

A foul fly catch depends on inning, score, and whether an outfielder is within safe throwing distance of home plate or the base at which the play is to be made.

When a fly ball is lost in the sun, an outfielder can locate it by taking one step to the right or left; this will bring the ball out of the sun.

Outfielders should follow the ball all the way from the pitcher's hand to the plate; this will help them to get a jump on the ball.

Outfielders should take a warm-up ball out with them at the start of every inning and play catch to keep their arms loose.

When you run after hard-hit balls, don't extend your glove hand until the last second.

When the pitcher is being hit hard, outfielders should play deep and cut back across the left center and right center alleys.

chapter 18
DODGERS' CUT-OFF PLAYS

Cut-off plays are team plays designed to make the team defense as sharp as possible. A common statement about the Dodgers teams from baseball people is that they "make errors but not mistakes." Here are the things they emphasize in team defense.

DEFENSIVE (CUT-OFF) PLAYS

Nobody on base, single to outfield

When the ball goes to left field, the shortstop goes to second base. The second baseman backs up the throw.

When the ball goes to center field, between the shortstop and the second baseman, one of these men calls the play.

When the ball goes to right field, the second baseman stays at second base. The shortstop backs up the throw.

Runner on first, single to outfield

When the ball goes to left field, the third baseman stays on the bag. The shortstop lines up the throw from the left-fielder to third base. The second baseman goes to second base; the first baseman goes to first base.

When the ball goes to center field, use the same set-up, except the shortstop lines up the throw from center field to third base, in a cut-off position.

When the ball goes to right field, use the same set-up, except the shortstop lines up the throw from right field to third base.

Runner on second, single to outfield

When the ball goes to left field, the third baseman cuts off the man on his way to the plate. The shortstop goes to third base. The second baseman stays at second base, and the first baseman stays at first base.

When the ball goes to center or right field, the first baseman cuts off the man on his way to the plate. The second baseman goes to first base. The shortstop goes to second base. The third baseman goes to third base.

When there is a ground single to left field that the third baseman chases, the first baseman is cut-off man.

Runner on third, sacrifice fly to outfield

Use the same cut-off positions as for the preceding play (runner on second, single to outfield).

Nobody on base, long single—possible double

When the ball goes to left field, beyond the left-fielder, the third baseman stays at third base. The shortstop goes to his cut-off position to line up the throw. The second baseman stays at second base and the first baseman stays at first.

When the ball goes to right field, beyond the right-fielder, the third baseman stays at third. The shortstop goes to second base. The second baseman goes to his cut-off position to line up the throw.

Nobody on base, sure double

When the ball goes to left center, the third baseman stays at third base. The shortstop lines up the throw to third in relay position. The second baseman backs up the shortstop and calls the play. The first baseman trails the base runner to second base for a possible pick-off from the relay man.

When the ball goes to right center, the third baseman stays at third base. The second baseman lines up the throw to third in the relay position. The shortstop backs up the second baseman and calls the play. The first baseman plays the same as when the ball goes to left center.

When the ball goes to the left field corner, the third baseman stays at his bag. The shortstop goes to the left field line in relay position. The second baseman goes to the left field line in a back-up position

to call the play. The first baseman trails the runner to second, as before.

When the ball goes to the right field corner, the third baseman goes to third base. The shortstop goes to the mound area to line up in cut-off position for the play at third, or the subsequent play at home. The second baseman and first baseman go to the right field line in relay and back-up positions. The one with the best relay arm handles the ball. The center-fielder and shortstop should be alert to cover second base as the play develops. The left-fielder should be alert to back up third base.

Runner on first, sure double

When the ball goes to left center, the third baseman, the shortstop, and the second baseman play the same as when no one is on base. The first baseman goes to the cut-off position around the mound. The right-fielder should be alert to cover second base.

When the ball goes to right center, the third baseman, the shortstop, and the second baseman play the same as when no one is on. The first baseman should be alert to cover second as the play develops. The left-fielder backs up third.

When the ball goes to the right field corner, the third baseman goes to third base. The shortstop and second baseman go to relay and back-up positions. The first baseman goes to the mound area in the cut-off position. The right-fielder and the center-fielder should be alert to cover second base.

When the ball goes to the right field corner, the third baseman stays at third base. The shortstop goes to the mound area to line up in the cut-off position for the play at third, or the subsequent play at home. The second baseman and first baseman go to the right field line in relay and back-up positions. The one with the best relay arm handles ball. The shortstop and the center-fielder should be alert to cover second base.

Catcher's defense on double steal drill

Look at the runner on third base, but throw to second base.

Throw back to the pitcher, but don't look at the runner on third. Get a sign from the pitcher acknowledging your sign.

Bluff a full throw to second base, but throw to third base.

Pitchout. Shortstop and second baseman leave their positions.

chapter 19
PRACTICE SESSIONS

Individual groups working on skills is an excellent way to improve.

It is most important for a coach to organize and plan practice and pregame practice. Such things as batting practice, game pitcher, bull pen pitcher, bull pen catchers, coaches, infield hitters, and who will hit fungos should be listed ahead of time.

SUGGESTED METHOD OF WORKOUTS

Pitchers

Have ball players loosen up by playing catch for ten or fifteen minutes, or by playing pepper. While this is going on, the pitcher who is to start throwing batting practice should warm up with a catcher. As soon as he is ready to pitch, practice should begin.

Work out a schedule for pitchers who are to work batting practice. Do not have pitchers throwing batting practice every day. Allow at least one day's rest between turns on the mound.

Allow a pitcher to work ten to fifteen minutes batting practice, and be certain that he works under game conditions. Be sure to have another pitcher loosening up while one is pitching practice, so that he will be available for replacement.

The pitcher should stress getting the ball over the plate for the batter's benefit.

The pitcher should alternate his stance on the rubber; winding up and pitching to one hitter, holding a man on base, and pitching to the next hitter. He also should learn the habit of breaking toward first base on all balls hit to his left. On most balls hit this way, he should take a step or two to get into the habit of breaking in direction of first base. Once in a while the coach should instruct the pitcher to complete his run to the bag to see how he makes the play and to correct any mistakes.

The pitcher generally cannot do hard work the day before a game and be a strong pitcher in the contest. A little pepper and a five-minute loosening-up period is sufficient. This is an individual condition, and each pitcher must know how much work is beneficial to him on the day before a game.

When a pitcher has completed his turn on the rubber, he should do lots of running. Short sprints of about fifty yards, and yards of hard running returning in a walk, will keep his legs and wind in shape. After the workout, if a pitcher is to be kept on the field, he should change his undershirt and put on a jacket. After pitching practice, lots of running, and playing pepper, it is best to dismiss the pitcher for the rest of the day if conditions allow it.

Batters

Once batting practice has started, there should not be more than two men around the cage awaiting their turn. The players should know their batting turn from the posted list. All other players should go to their respective positions.

The batter should be made to bunt one and hit three. He should run on the last hit at top speed. When he reaches second base, he returns to his position. As the next batter steps in to hit, another player runs in toward the cage immediately and starts to swing bats so he will be ready to take his turn.

By constant hustling, a club can get in several rounds in the time allotted for batting practice.

During batting practice, put a runner on second; call the situation at no outs. Work with hitters to move this runner to third. Try to get batters to hit sacrifice flies or ground balls to the right side of the infield to get the runner into scoring position.

Infielders and Outfielders

Station all players at their positions. Coach stands at home plate and hits the ball anywhere in the field; this challenges the team's defense and sets up any situation that could come up in a game. Three outs clears the bases. Have four base runners available. The coach may set the inning, score and situation. This is one of the finest defensive baseball drills possible. It allows the team to work on all situations: bunts, hotboxes, cut-off plays, rundowns, double steals, squeeze, relays, and the hit and run.

Coach takes each player, one at a time, and hits fungos of all types to him for fifteen minutes; he hits grounders at him to his left, right, and in front of him and has him throw to first. This is a good conditioner and skills teacher.

The coach stands near the batting cage, which enables him to watch and instruct the batter, pitcher, and catcher. He can be hitting ground balls to one or two infielders, who can complete throws to first base or practice the double play.

Another player can be at the opposite side of the cage hitting to an infielder who makes the play and rolls the ball back to him. He concentrates on learning to field ground balls properly.

The infield hitters should time their batting so that it comes immediately after the batter at the plate has just taken his swing. This is to avoid having the infielder watch two balls at the same time.

BAD THROW TO FIRST

Second base and shortstop should constantly practice handling the ball and making pivots.

Two other players can be used, one on the left field line and the other on the right field line. They fungo balls to outfielders, both fly balls and grounders.

The catchers, wearing shinguards and gear, throw erratic one-hop pegs to each other for fifteen minutes to get the timing of the ball bouncing off the ground.

Wind up the practice session by devoting fifteen minutes to outfield and infield practice. The outfielders should practice making throws to second base, third base, and home plate, always from their other work positions.

An additional fifteen minutes could be spent on any other individual or team weaknesses, such as base running, pitching, covering first base, fielding bunts, etc.

The day after a game, the coach should discuss all the possible errors of judgment that occurred during the game. Always remember that lack of experience is the cause of most mistakes. A coach should not make any public criticism of the players' mistakes on the field.

PITCHERS' DRILLS

Here are some general suggestions.

Pitchers must learn to cover first base at all times when a ball is hit to their left. Early in the season pitchers should take infield practice with the team; players should hit the ball to the pitcher every trip around the horn. Practice on first base and pitcher teamwork.

The pitcher must also learn to charge the third base foul line with men on first and second and none out. The pitcher must learn how to work the double play on balls hit back to him. These situations should be practiced.

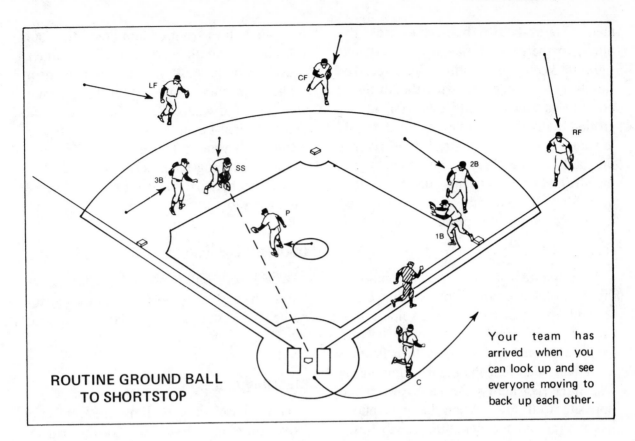

ROUTINE GROUND BALL
TO SHORTSTOP

Your team has
arrived when you
can look up and see
everyone moving to
back up each other.

To aid a pitcher in his throwing practice, place a tape from his pivot foot to the rubber and make him throw his forward leg across the line. This keeps him from throwing across his own body, opens his hips up, and achieves maximum smoothness and power.

Grass Drill

The pitcher reaches as far back as possible in a wind-up and follows down and through, trying to pick up some grass on the field or a ball lying on the ground as his pitching arm comes over, down, and around. This drill should be repeated fifty times. It teaches reach-back and follow-through.

A variation of this is done with a line of baseballs in front of the pitcher. As his arm sweeps down, he picks up one of the balls, brings his arm up and back, and begins his pitch again, sweeping down, re-leasing the ball, and picking up another one from the ground. He becomes, in effect, a pitching windmill.

Pick-up Drill

This drill, while used a lot with pitchers, is also fine for the whole team to condition them and sharpen their skills at fielding bunts or topped grounders. It involves two

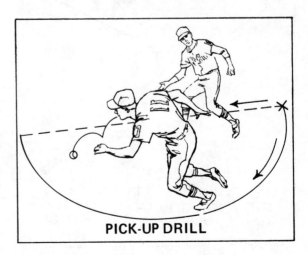

PICK-UP DRILL

men. One rolls two balls, one after the other, to the second man, to his left and right to keep him hustling. The receiver stands in a direct line with the thrower, not too far away, and runs to field the ground balls as first one is rolled to his left and then one to his right. He returns the balls to the thrower and they repeat the drill. Try this twenty times the first day, forty the second, and one hundred from then on during spring training.

Fungo Drill

Used mainly for pitchers as a conditioning drill, this exercise involves a fungo hitter and up to ten men. The ten line up on the left or right foul line, fairly far beyond the infield, and each takes a turn fielding a hit ball. The first man starts running as fast as he can across the field toward the opposite foul line. When he gets about halfway across the field, the fungo hitter

bats the ball in front of him down the foul line he is running toward. The runner must catch the ball. As each man in turn makes this run, he lines up on the opposite foul line, and when all men have made the run, the drill begins again with the fungo hitter hitting along the other foul line and the men running back across the field.

Use pitchers as fungo hitters. It is good for their shoulders.

DOUBLE PLAY DRILLS

Coach rolls ball to shortstop and second baseman and they practice working together with the first baseman on double plays.

STEALING DRILL

Have base runners time the pitcher's move; three to four seconds for the ball to

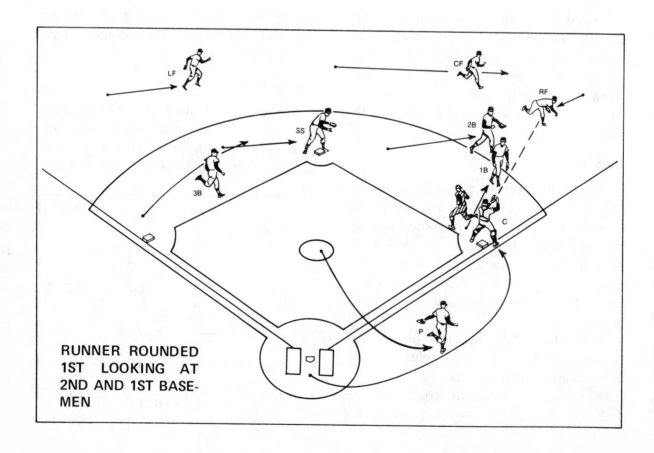

RUNNER ROUNDED 1ST LOOKING AT 2ND AND 1ST BASEMEN

BURMA ROAD

This is one of the very best conditioning drills.

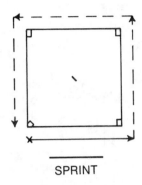 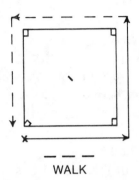

———— SPRINT

– – – – WALK

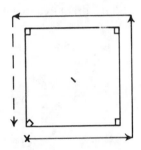 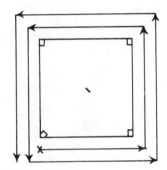

1. Players sprint to first, form a single line and walk around bases until the first man touches home.
2. Sprint to second and walk to home.
3. Sprint to third and walk home.
4. Sprint around all bases twice.
5. Optional method: use sprint around all bases four times.

Boys don't really realize how far they are running. They like the competition of this drill, and it gets them in splendid shape.

---

reach the plate is time enough to steal home if the runner is fast.

TEAM CONDITIONING DRILL: BURMA ROAD

This is one of the very best conditioning drills. The players sprint to first, form a single line and walk around the bases until the first man in the line touches home. Leading the line, he then sprints to second base and walks home; then sprints to third and walks home; and finally sprints around all the bases twice (or more, depending on the coach's instructions).

Boys don't realize how far they are running; they like the competition of this drill and it gets them in splendid shape.

DEFENSIVE FIELD POSITIONS

Against an Extreme Pull Hitter

(Field positions shown for right-handed pull hitter; shift positions to other side of field for left-handed pull hitter.)

Power Shift

These field positions defend against a

long ball hitter; note the four-man outfield.

Bunt Defense

The seven man infield; runners on first
and second, no one out.

Runner on first, no one out. It is advisable to have the second baseman charging and in position between first base and
home because the first baseman is generally taller and much more adept at catching thrown balls, and can therefore cover
first base better than the second baseman.

The following illustration is one that has
proved very successful in high school and
American Legion baseball.

Seven Man Infield—runners on first and
second and none out.

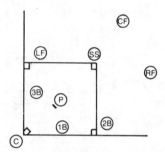

Power Shift—great long ball hitter, no one on
(four man outfield).

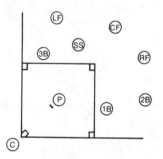

Bunt Defense—with only runner on first base,
none out:

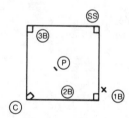

It is advisable to have second baseman
charging and in position between first base
and home because first baseman is generally taller and much more adept at catching thrown balls.

chapter 20

SITUATION DRILLS

SITUATION 1: DEFENSIVE PLAYS

No one on base.
Batter singles to either (A) left, (B) center, or (C) right.

Pitcher: Moves to a position halfway between mound and 2nd.

Catcher: Follows runner down to 1st base.

1st Baseman: Makes sure the runner tags the base in making the turn and then covers 1st base.

Shortstop: Covers 2nd to take throw from left fielder with 2nd baseman backing him up.

2nd Baseman: Covers 2nd to take throw from right fielder with shortstop backing him up.

Single to Center: Whoever is closer to 2nd base covers with the other man backing up the play if able.

3rd Baseman: On single to right, backs up shortstop on throw to 2nd base.

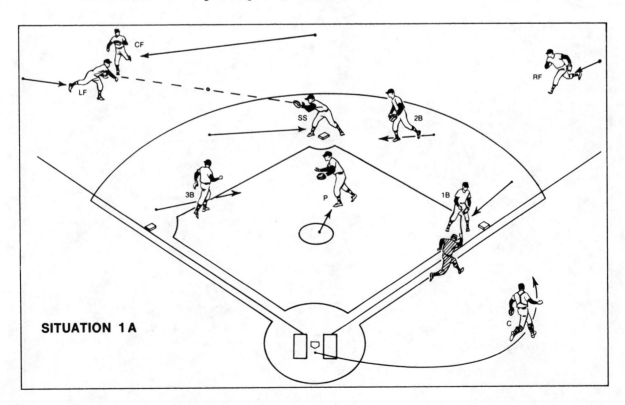

SITUATION 1A

Outfielders:
  (a) Center fielder backs up left fielder and right fielder moves in toward 1st base.
  (b) Left and right fielders back up center fielder.
  (c) Center fielder backs up right fielder and left fielder moves in toward 3rd base.

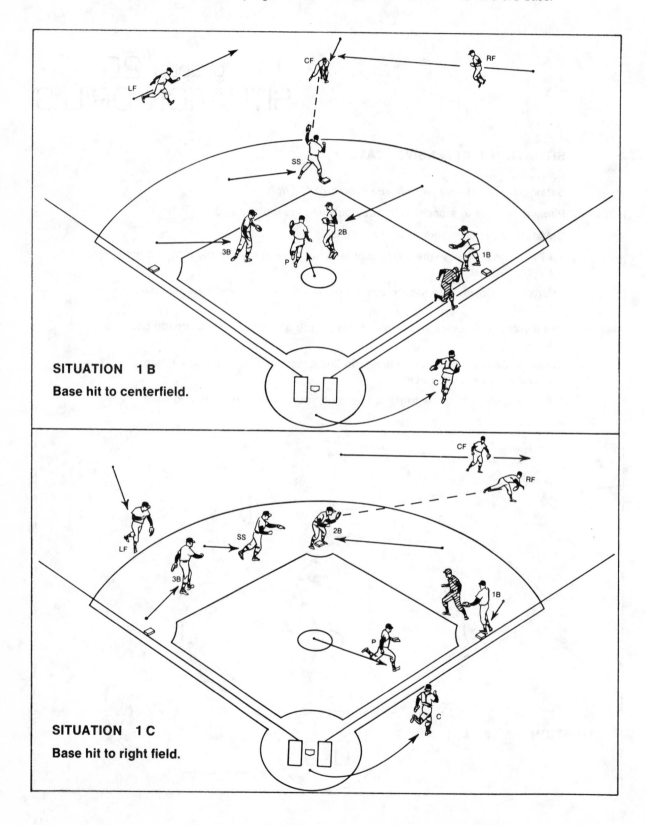

SITUATION   1 B

Base hit to centerfield.

SITUATION   1 C

Base hit to right field.

SITUATION 2

No one on base (or)
Man on 3rd or 2nd (or)
Men on 3rd and 2nd bases.
Batter hits a sure double, possible triple, into left center.

Pitcher: Backs up 3rd base in line with throw.

Catcher: Protects home plate.

1st Baseman: Trails the runner to 2nd base and covers the bag, ready for a play if runner rounds base too far.

2nd Baseman: Trails about 30 feet behind shortstop in line with 3rd base.

Shortstop: Goes to a spot in left center to become relay man.

3rd Baseman: Covers 3rd base and stands on left field side of base.

Left Fielder: Backs up the center fielder.

Right Fielder: Moves in toward 2nd base.

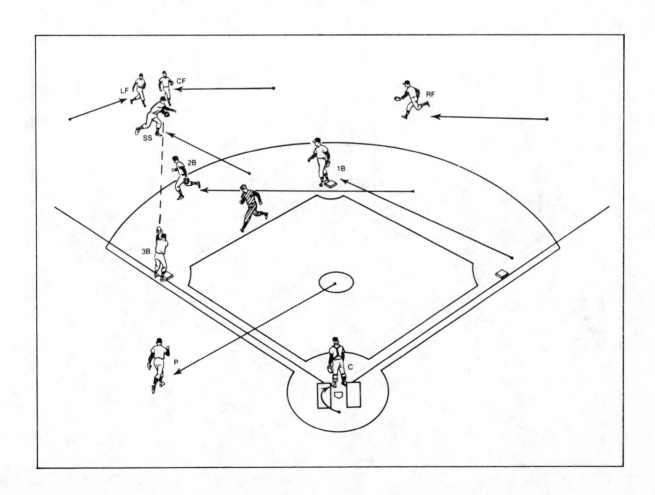

SITUATION 3A

No one on base (or)
Man on 3rd base or 2nd (or)
Men on 3rd and 2nd bases.
Batter hits a sure double, possible triple, just to the right of the center fielder.

Pitcher: Backs up 3rd base. Gets as deep as possible.

Catcher: Protects home plate.

1st Baseman: Trails the runner to 2nd base and covers the bag ready for a play at that base.

2nd Baseman: Goes to spot in center field, in line with 3rd, to become relay man.

Shortstop: Trails about 30 feet behind 2nd baseman in line with 3rd base.

3rd Baseman: Covers 3rd base.

Left Fielder: Moves in toward 3rd base.

Right Fielder: Backs up center fielder on ball hit to right center. On ball hit to left center, moves in toward 1st base.

SITUATION 3B
(exception to standard rule for trailer on 2 & 3)

Man on 1st base (or)
Men on 1st and 2nd base.
Batter hits a sure double or possible triple into right center—a chance to throw out runner from 1st at the plate.

Pitcher: Goes halfway between 3rd and plate to see where the throw is coming and then backs up either base.

Catcher: Covers home plate.

1st Baseman: Cut-off man about 45 feet from home plate.

2nd Baseman: Is the relay man to either home or 3rd.

Shortstop: Covers 2nd base.

3rd Baseman: Covers 3rd base.

Left Fielder: Moves into area behind 3rd base.

Right Fielder: Backs up center fielder.

SITUATION 4

Man on 1st base (or)
Men on 3rd and 1st.
Batter singles to the outfield.

Pitcher: Backs up 3rd base in line with throw.

Catcher: Protects home plate.

1st Baseman: Covers 1st base. Makes sure runner tags 1st base.

2nd Baseman: Covers 2nd base. Makes sure runner tags 2nd base.

Shortstop: Stations himself about 45 feet from 3rd base, on a direct line from 3rd base to the outfielder fielding the ball.

3rd Baseman: Covers 3rd base.

Left Fielder: On ball hit to right field, moves in toward 3rd base.

Center Fielder: Backs up right or left fielder, wherever ball is hit.

Right Fielder: On ball hit to left field, moves in toward 1st base. Backs up center fielder on balls hit to right of the center fielder.

SITUATION 5

Man on 2nd base (or)
Men on 2nd and 3rd bases.
Batter singles to right field—chance to get runner from 2nd at home.

Pitcher: Backs up home plate.

Catcher: Covers home plate.

1st Baseman: Takes position about 45 feet from home plate to become cut-off man.

2nd Baseman: Covers 1st base.

Shortstop: Covers 2nd base.

3rd Baseman: Covers 3rd base.

Left Fielder: Moves in toward 2nd base.

Center Fielder: Backs up right fielder.

Right Fielder: Makes low, hard throw toward the cut-off man.

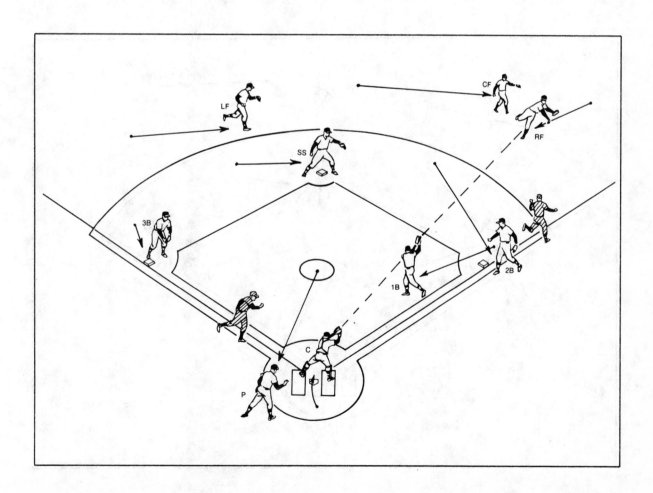

SITUATION 6A

Man on 2nd base (or)
Men on 2nd and 3rd bases.
Batter singles to left or center field—chance to get runner from 2nd at home.

Pitcher: Backs up home plate.

Catcher: Covers home plate.

1st Baseman: Remains on 1st base on all hits to left and center except when 1st base is occupied. If ball is hit to center, then he is the cut-off man.

2nd Baseman: Covers 2nd base.

Shortstop: Covers 3rd base.

3rd Baseman: Takes a position about 45 feet from home plate to become the cut-off man if no runner is on 1st base.

Left Fielder: Makes low, hard throw to cut-off man on hits to left. Backs up center fielder on balls hit to center.

Center Fielder: Backs up left fielder on balls hit to left field.

Right Fielder: Backs up center fielder on balls hit to center. Moves in toward 2nd base on balls hit to left field.

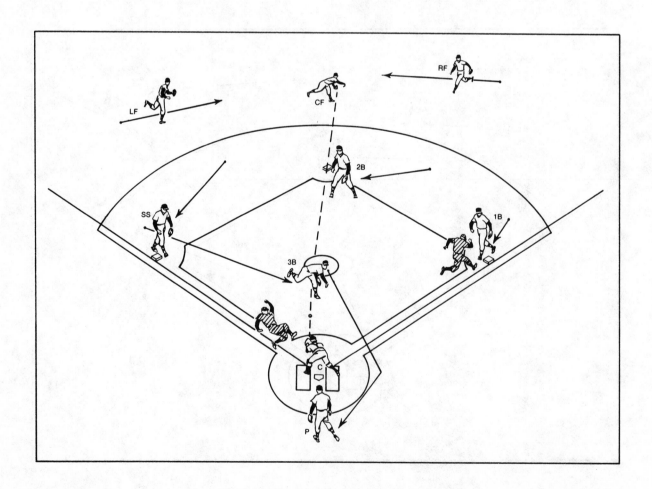

SITUATION 6B
(exception to standard rule)

Men on 1st and 2nd (or)
Men on 1st, 2nd, and 3rd.
Batter singles to center field—chance to get runner from 2nd at the plate.

Pitcher: Backs up home plate or goes in between to see where throw is made.

Catcher: Covers home plate.

1st Baseman: Moves into a spot 45 feet from home plate in line with the throw to be cut-off man.

2nd Baseman: If possible goes and covers 1st base.

Shortstop: Covers 2nd base.

3rd Baseman: Covers 3rd base.

Left Fielder: Backs up center fielder.

Right Fielder: Backs up center fielder.

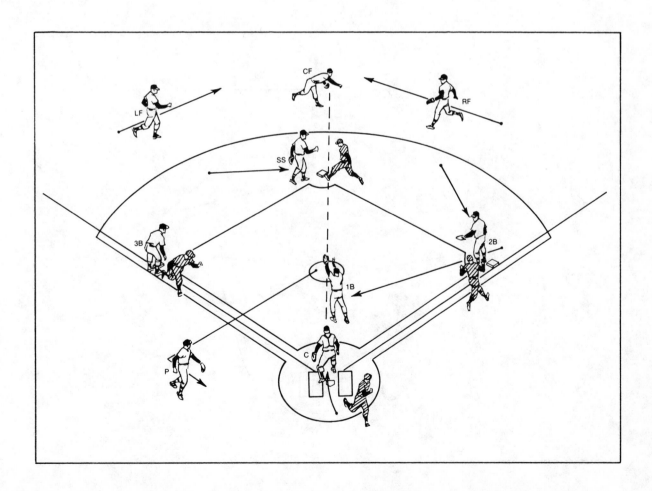

SITUATION 7A
(exception to standard rule)

Man on 2nd base (or)
Men on 2nd and 3rd bases.
Batter singles on ground between 1st and 2nd basemen into right field—chance to get runner from 2nd at home plate.

Pitcher: Starts to cover 1st and then retreats to cover or back up home plate.

Catcher: Covers home plate.

1st Baseman: After attempting to field ball, continues to cover 2nd base.

2nd Baseman: Covers 1st base.

3rd Baseman: Cut-off man. Takes spot about 45 feet from home plate in a line between the right fielder and home.

Shortstop: Covers 3rd base.

Left Fielder: Moves into area behind 3rd base.

Center Fielder: Backs up right fielder, moves in toward 2nd base after ball is fielded.

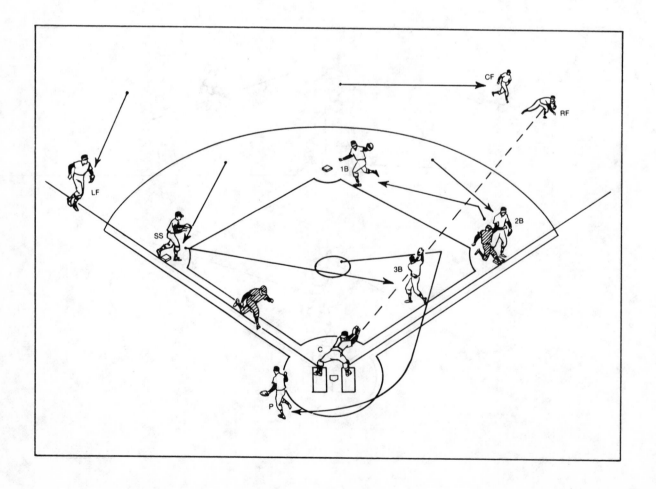

SITUATION 7B
(exception to standard rule)

Men on 1st and 2nd—double play in order.
*Batter singles on ground between 1st and 2nd into right field—chance to get man
from 2nd at the plate.*

Pitcher: Starts to cover 1st base, and when ball gets through, he retreats to
become the cut-off man.

Catcher: Covers home plate.

1st Baseman: When he can't field the ball, he is out of the play.

2nd Baseman: Covers 1st base.

Shortstop: Covers 2nd base.

3rd Baseman: Covers 3rd base.

Left Fielder: Moves into area behind 3rd to back up.

Center Fielder: Backs up right fielder.

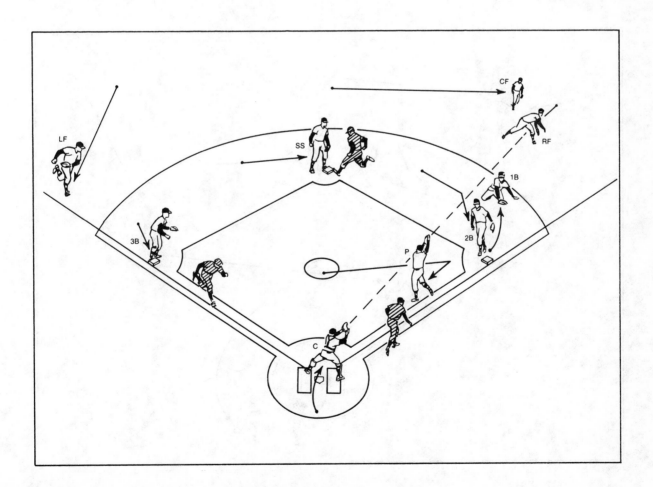

SITUATION 7C
(exception to standard rule)

Man on 2nd base (or)
Men on 2nd and 3rd bases.
Batter singles in the hole between shortstop and 3rd baseman into left field.
Chance to get runner from 2nd at the plate.

Pitcher: Backs up home plate.

Catcher: Covers home plate.

1st Baseman: Cut-off man. Takes a position about 45 feet from home plate in line with left fielder and home plate.

2nd Baseman: Covers 2nd base.

Shortstop: May have to cover 3rd base if 3rd baseman cannot recover.

3rd Baseman: Covers 3rd base if possible.

Left Fielder: Makes low throw to the plate.

Center Fielder: Backs up left fielder.

Right Fielder: Comes in quickly to try to cover 1st base.

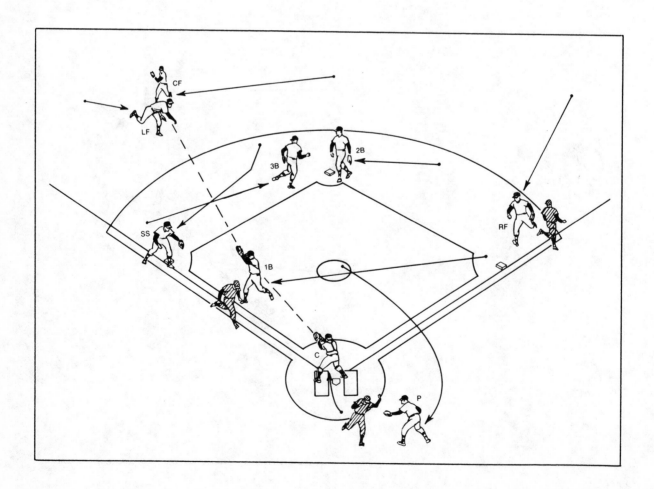

SITUATION 8

Man on 1st base.
Batter hits double, possible triple, down right field foul line—chance to get runner at home.

Pitcher: Backs up home.

Catcher: Covers home plate.

1st Baseman: Trails 2nd baseman. Remains about 30 feet back.

2nd Baseman: Relay man. Goes to a spot in right field along foul line in line with right fielder and home.

Shortstop: Covers 2nd base.

3rd Baseman: Covers 3rd base.

Left Fielder: Moves in toward 3rd base.

Center Fielder: Backs up right fielder.

SITUATION 9

Men on 1st and 2nd (or)
Bases loaded.
Tying run is on 1st. Single to right field.
This is a judgment play. Always keep tying or winning run from going to 3rd if less than 2 out.

Pitcher: Backs up 3rd.

Catcher: Covers home plate.

1st Baseman: Remains on 1st.

2nd Baseman: Covers 2nd.

Shortstop: Gets in line with throw and is relay man.

3rd Baseman: Covers 3rd.

Left Fielder: Moves in to a point near the line and backs up 3rd.

Center Fielder: Backs up right fielder.

Right Fielder: Makes a low throw to the shortstop who is cut-off man.

Give opposing team two runs to keep the tying run at 2nd base in this situation.

SITUATION 10

Man on 2nd base.
Hitter is the tying run.
Single to left field.

Pitcher: Moves off mound to back up home plate in case the left fielder makes the throw home.

Catcher: Covers home plate.

1st Baseman: Covers 1st base.

2nd Baseman: Backs up 2nd base.

Shortstop: Covers 2nd base.

3rd Baseman: Moves into position to be cut-off man in case the left fielder throws home.

Left Fielder: Makes low throw to 2nd base to keep batter from advancing into scoring position.

Center Fielder: Backs up left fielder.

Right Fielder: Moves into position to help back up 2nd base.

Never let the tying run get into scoring position at 2nd base by making a foolish throw to the plate.

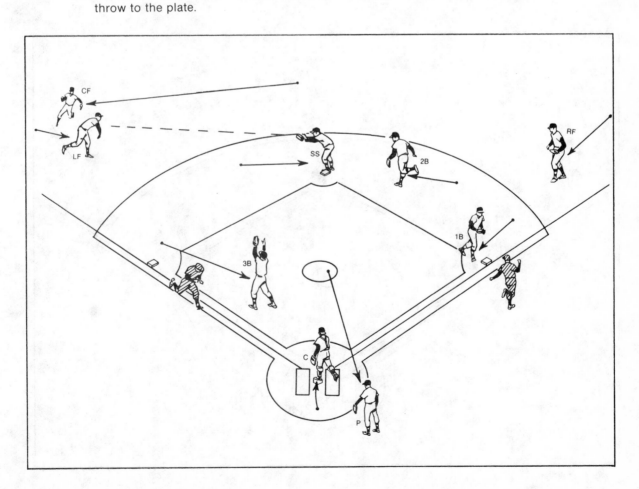

SITUATION 11
(defense against item 2 in important offensive situations)

Runners on 1st and 3rd.
Less than 2 out.
Foul fly is hit behind the plate.
Both runners tag up, and runner on 1st breaks for 2nd. If there is no cut-off man,
the runner on 3rd will score if throw goes through to 2nd base from catcher.

Pitcher: Covers home plate.

Catcher: Catches pop-up and throws to cut-off man.

1st Baseman: Helps on pop-up.

2nd Baseman: Becomes cut-off man behind pitching mound.

Shortstop: Covers 2nd base.

3rd Baseman: Covers 3rd base.

Left Fielder: Comes in to help back up at short.

Center Fielder: Backs up 2nd.

Right Fielder: Covers 1st base.

SITUATION 12

Runners on 1st and 3rd and none out.
A pop fly is hit behind 1st base.
Both runners tag up, and the runner on 1st breaks for 2nd.

Pitcher: Comes to a point halfway between mound and 1st base to be the cut-off man.

Catcher: Covers home plate.

1st Baseman: Catches the pop-up and throws it to the pitcher.

2nd Baseman: Also is going after the pop-up and then hustles to cover 1st.

Shortstop: Covers 2nd base.

3rd Baseman: Covers 3rd base.

Left Fielder: Moves into an area behind 3rd for back-up man.

Center Fielder: Backs up 2nd base.

Right Fielder: Moves in to help catch the pop-up.

DEFENSIVE ASSIGNMENTS ON BUNT SITUATIONS

SITUATION 13A

With a runner on 1st base and the bunt in order.

Pitcher: Breaks toward plate after delivering the ball.

Catcher: Fields all bunts possible, calls the play, and covers 3rd base when 3rd baseman fields the ball in close to home plate.

1st Baseman: Covers the area between 1st and the mound.

2nd Baseman: Covers 1st base. Cheats by shortening position.

Shortstop: Covers 2nd base.

3rd Baseman: Covers the area between 3rd and the mound.

Left Fielder: Moves in toward 2nd base area.

Center Fielder: Backs up 2nd base.

Right Fielder: Backs up 1st base.

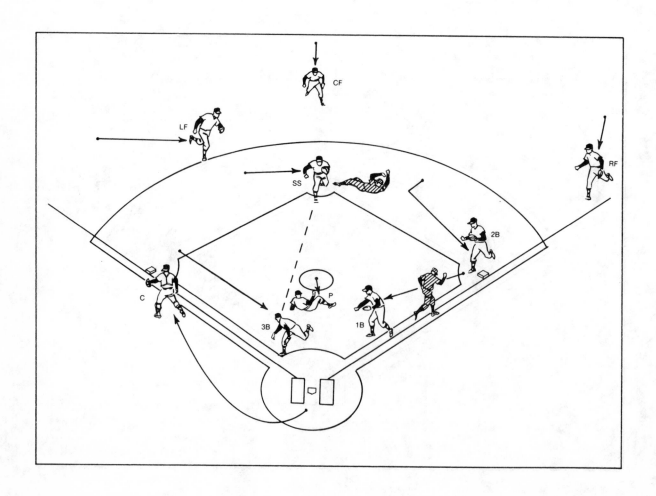

SITUATION 13B

With runners on 1st and 2nd—bunt situation in order.

Pitcher: Breaks toward 3rd base line upon delivering the ball.

Catcher: Fields bunts in front of plate: *calls the play.*

1st Baseman: Responsible for all balls in the area between 1st and a direct line from the mound to home.

2nd Baseman: Covers 1st base.

Shortstop: Holds runner close to bag before pitch and covers 2nd base.

3rd Baseman: Takes position on the edge of the grass and calls the play—whether the pitcher or 3rd baseman is to field the bunt.

Left Fielder: Backs up 3rd base.

Center Fielder: Backs up 2nd base.

Right Fielder: Backs up 1st base.

Note: First objective is to retire the runner at 3rd, but 1 runner *must* be retired.

chapter 21
WHAT MAKES A MAJOR LEAGUER?

Recently, one of the top sportswriters in Cleveland, Dennis Lustig, got me to thinking by saying, "You're always coaching young people in the major league way of playing baseball. *What is the major league way of playing baseball?*"

Playing baseball the major league way is a way to learn the fundamental skills properly, which will take you to the top of your profession, into the major leagues, if you have the talent and desire. If you're the worst shortstop in the major leagues, that means you're one of the top thirty men in the world at your profession; quite an accomplishment. The major league way of playing baseball will take you as close to perfection as your abilities and desire will allow you to develop.

The major league way of playing baseball can be taught to kids from age six on up. (Taiwan Little League team good example.) You might as well learn the big league way of doing things from your youngest years on. Notice the perfect ma-

jor league form of some of the youngsters in this book. Besides learning baseball the major league way, *have fun playing the game.*

We've tried to teach you the major league way of playing baseball in these pages. Now it's up to you to put all of your courage, desire, love of the game, hard work, poise, conditioning, and talent into playing baseball the major league way. Work hard and get the most out of your God-given abilities. Give it your best.

Ten years ago I penned the following words about Mel Stottlemyre and what it takes to become a major leaguer. Nothing has changed in this respect. Mel became one of the greatest pitchers in baseball during the sixties and early seventies. Not only that, but just as important, he is a real gentleman and a big league human being. Today he is a pitching coach for the Seattle Mariner organization.

The words to follow may give you an insight into what makes a major leaguer as he is growing up. Try to incorporate these values into your life if you want to get to the top.

Vern Ruhle, whom I had the pleasure of coaching in his early years, is a carbon copy of Mel. Both had that burning desire to become the best in their field. They had poise to such a point that if the stadium fell down, they would back off the rubber, wait for it to settle, and then look in for the sign. They had ability to overcome injury and come back. Mel's career ended when he came back too soon from an injury because the Yankees were in the middle of a pennant race. Vern came back in a late season pennant race last year from back surgery in the spring and pitched effectively for the Astros, as they made a run at the Reds in 1979.

In August 1964 the New York Yankees were in third place and the pitching staff was riddled, their spirits low. At this time the Yankees called up a young right-hander named Mel Stottlemyre from Richmond, a Triple-A farm team. Mel rattled off nine wins and three losses and a sharp 2.16 E.R.A. He topped this off with three World Series starts and one win in the fall classic. At the age of twenty-two he had had more thrills than the average person has in a lifetime. This young man made the American dream come true.

When I first met Mel in 1959 there were several things which impressed me a great deal. First was his ability to throw a baseball so it would naturally sink—even his fast ball would sink. In all the years I have played and coached, I have seen only about six people who could do this. The basic philosophy of pitching in pro ball is to keep the ball low. Very few home runs are hit on pitches around the knees. Here was a youngster who could keep the ball low and more important his low pitches

all moved. From the first workout, I felt Mel was a lad who could go all the way to the top with the tools he had. A coach's dream come true, a chance to work with a boy who, barring injury, had the potential to reach the major leagues.

Many successful pitchers have had the natural gift of large hands and long fingers. As you can see by the pictures, Mel also possessed this gift. Another pitcher with this gift is Sandy Koufax; he could hold seven baseballs in one hand. Hans Lobert, a former coach of the Giants, tells that the legendary Walter Johnson was the only man he ever saw who could scratch his knees without bending over. These pitchers' phenomenal speed was partly due to their long, long arms, large hands and long fingers.

Another quality Mel has is a burning competitive drive to be the best in his field. He is one of the best competitors I have ever had the pleasure of working with. All the great ones have this burning desire for excellence. Dave Kosher, a major league scout, once said that our job would be easy if we could see what is under a boy's shirt. We can clock a boy's speed, we can see how well he throws and hits, but what we really want to know is what he will do in a clutch situation: bases loaded, two outs, does he get the hitter or does he fold? Mel has this clutch performance trait in abundance.

Another attribute that impressed me was Mel's effort to improve himself and his pitching. This is one of the most important reasons for his fast rise in the baseball world. If he pitched a two-hit shutout, he would immediately set out to improve on his last effort. He is always looking at his performance critically. A few years ago we were making a color film on how to pitch for the local youth in the area of Sunnyside, Washington. The first thing

Mel said was, "Check the films over and over. Run them in slow motion to see if you can read me." (Reading a pitcher means getting clues from his style about which pitch he is getting ready to throw: throwing his different pitches with different arm angles, showing more white of the ball with one pitch than with another, exhibiting any small telltale mannerism that will tip off the hitter to the pitch he's about to receive.)

The Mel Stottlemyre story started in Mabton, a small town in central Washington. There Mel played little league, pony league, American Legion, high school, and Spanish League baseball. In high school he also played football and was an outstanding basketball player—as well as being president of the student body.

It was in Mabton that Mel developed a real love for fishing and hunting—two hobbies that help keep him in splendid shape during the off-season. (Have you noticed how many athletes have a big interest in hunting and fishing? From those years in Mabton, Mel has always kept in training. He neither drinks nor smokes. He is a fine example for boys just starting in baseball.

Mel has two brothers and one sister. His parents have always followed their boys' activities with interest and enthusiasm and given them valuable encouragement. Mr. and Mrs. Stottlemyre attended all Mel's games whenever possible. Parents' interest is a big booster for young players; it is surprising how few parents really take an interest at this critical stage of their children's development. Sad to say, I have coached many boys who had much ability but never developed their potential either as baseball players or as people because no one took an early interest in them.

During his formative years, Mel devel-

oped the confidence and coolness under pressure that has been his trademark in the big leagues. He has the feeling that he can get any batter out who steps into the box, and he proceeds to do his job with neat dispatch.

Mel Stottlemyre shows his fine pitching form.

The highest compliment that Mel has received is that he is a player in the true Yankee tradition. The intangible that makes the Yankees different from other teams is that everyone is really pulling for everyone else. When Mel first came up, the pitcher who helped him and gave him his own book on all the hitters in the league was Ralph Terry, the pitcher whose job Mel was taking over. Tony Kubek, in spring training, worked with the shortstops, telling them everything he knew, even though they were trying to take his job. This is the Yankee spirit, the same spirit Mel has known all of his life. He is never in too great a hurry to help a youngster or drop a line to an inquiring coach about how he throws his famous sinker. Mel Stottlemyre's cap size is the same today as it was many years ago when he pitched in the Lower Valley baseball parks in Washington. Mel still displays the love of the game as he did as a youngster.

Mel, who is 6 feet 2 inches tall and weighs 185 pounds, started out as a side-arm pitcher. Later he developed into a three-quarter delivery pitcher. Then he developed into an almost straight overhand pitcher for two reasons: it is easier to get your body into an overhand delivery, and an overhand delivery makes it easier to get more on your curve ball. Mel has always been able to throw his fast ball with a natural sinking movement, which makes it doubly tough to hit. The sinker is thrown with a cross action in the fingers and wrist, but Mel has had a natural sinker from the first time I saw him step on the mound. He has worked and developed his curve ball until it is a sharp down-breaking curve. His change-of-pace was developed by Jim Konstanty, former major league pitcher and pitching coach who taught Mel a unique change-up in which the pressure is applied by the second knuckle of the third finger and thumb; there is no pressure from the first two

fingers. It is delivered as if you were pulling down a window shade. Basically, though, Mel's money pitch is still the sinker ball.

He has developed control with the same footprint rhythm, and after warming up for fifteen minutes there is still only one left footprint, which is the mark of a pitcher who has developed a groove in his pitching motion. Mel's pattern for pitching is to keep the ball low, which is of prime importance and the key to successful pitching. One interesting thing about sinker-ball pitching is that if Mel hasn't pitched for quite a while, he will throw hard for two days before his starting assignment. If he doesn't, he will become too strong, and his sinker ball will straighten out instead of breaking down. Mel strongly endorses the use of John Sain's Spinner. Sain was the pitching coach for the Yankees and did an outstanding job. Mel uses a spinning drill, even while on the sidelines. This helps him develop the curve ball. He simply flips a baseball out of his open hand, as you would do in clicking your thumb and second finger together.

Mel Stottlemyre is living proof that talent is where you find it: anywhere. It is our hope that this book will help you in teaching or playing baseball whether it be in a vacant lot or on a regulation diamond.

index